A problem well put is half-solved. The reactionary is a man of few words, well-chosen, which cut to the heart of a problem. In the history of ideas there have been works which have laid bare the problems of modernity, and whose elegance has pointed the way to their solution.

Imperium Press' Studies in Reaction series distills the essence of reactionary thought. The series presents in compact format those seminal works which need so few words to say so much about modernity.

Joseph de Maistre was one of the strongest voices in 18th and 19th century reaction. Born into minor Savoyard nobility in 1753, he enjoyed a distinguished law career until he fled the French Republic's annexation, whereupon he acted as chief magistrate to Charles-Emmanuel's Sardinian court, later attaining a number of high offices. Maistre distinguished himself as a political commentator in *Considerations on France*, publishing many works over his life to great acclaim, particularly the posthumous *St. Petersburg Dialogues*.

ON THE
SPANISH
INQUISITION

JOSEPH
DE MAISTRE

Translated and with notes by
JOHN FLETCHER

PERTH
IMPERIUM PRESS
2022

Published by Imperium Press

www.imperiumpress.org

Letters on the Spanish Inquisition
published by W. Hughes 1838

All rights are reserved. No part of this publication may be reproduced, stored in a retrieval system, or transmitted in any form or by any means, electronic, mechanical, photocopying, recording, or otherwise, without prior permission of Imperium Press. Enquiries concerning reproduction outside the scope of the above should be directed to Imperium Press.

FIRST EDITION

A catalogue record for this
book is available from the
National Library of Australia

ISBN 978-1-922602-61-9 Paperback
ISBN 978-1-922602-62-6 E-book

Imperium Press has no responsibility for the persistence or accuracy of URLs for external or third-party Internet websites referred to in this publication and does not guarantee that any content on such websites is, or will remain, accurate or appropriate.

CONTENTS

Preface	vii
ON THE SPANISH INQUISITION	
First Letter	3
The Second Letter	27
The Third Letter	43
The Fourth Letter	59
The Fifth Letter	75

Preface

THE name of the Count Joseph De Maistre is a name which was long well known, and is still honoured, in the circles of statesmen and in the schools of diplomacy. In both of these he long acted a conspicuous part. During a considerable number of years he held, in his own country, the highest offices of state—was successively, Minister of Justice, Chancellor, &c.—conciliating, by the wisdom and prudence of his conduct, the universal esteem and approbation of the nation. Subsequently, he was appointed and sent, Ambassador to the Court of St. Petersburg, where he continued to reside during the long term of fourteen years—admired for his great talents and beloved for his amiable virtues. He died in 1822. The present accomplished Duchess of Laval is his daughter.

In the walks of literature, the Count is alike distinguished as he was in the schools of politics. His works are various and numerous. And if, indeed, the display of talents, eloquence, and learning—if originality, and refinement, of sentiment; if close reasoning, and sound philosophy, are the characteristics of interesting and useful works—it may confidently be asserted that there are few authors whose writings better deserve these praises than those of the Count De Maistre. His works are, for the most part, political. But they are, all of them, devoted to the cause of humanity, and to the interests of religion.

The work which he published at the beginning of the French Revolution, entitled, "*Considérations sur La France*," attracted—like that of our Burke, upon the same subject—universal attention and curiosity, insomuch that, although the Revolutionists employed every effort to suppress its circulation, it still, in the course of one year, passed through three editions. Another work of the Count's, entitled "*Du Pape*" is, again, a monument of great political wisdom, and of splendid eloquence and erudition. It has been pronounced by one of the first geniuses of Europe—the celebrated Mons. Bonald—"a sublime work." Whence also in France, Germany, and Italy, it has been everywhere read and extolled. Little inferior to this is his beautiful and learned work, "*Les Soirées de Saint Pétersbourg.*" If in this country the writings of the Count are little known, it is owing to the prevalence of those illiberal prejudices which withhold the Protestant from reading anything which tends, or appears to tend, to the defence of the Catholic religion.

The *Letters*, which I now present to the public, were addressed to a Russian nobleman, who, it appears, entertained all those same notions, and that same abhorrence, of the Inquisition, which in this country are so deeply imprinted on the public mind. He wrote them at the request of his noble friend, who, although so strongly prejudiced against the tribunal, was still willing and desirous to be instructed. They were written in the year 1815—that is, three years after the suppression of the Inquisition by the Revolutionary Cortes; and in the year of its re-establishment by Ferdinand—whence, also, he speaks of it as, at that time, actually existing. But, in order to satisfy his friend that the accounts which he gives of it are not the dictates of any partiality, he borrows a great part of the authorities and documents which he cites from the official reports themselves, of the Committee of the Cortes—that is, from the testimonials of the men who had abolished the Institution; and who, therefore, were its bitterest enemies. The concessions of such persons in its favour are, of course, arguments which cannot reasonably be suspected.

The Count divides the subject of his instructions into five separate *Letters*, of which the following are the brief and general outlines.

In the First, he shows that the Inquisition is not, in the first place, a purely ecclesiastical tribunal; secondly, that the Ecclesiastics, who do form a portion of its members, never, on any occasion, concur in the sentence which condemns any criminal to death; thirdly, that they never condemn any one for any mere or simple opinion; fourthly, that the tribunal is a completely royal institution, conducted under the control, and regulated by the will, of the monarch.

In the Second, he points out the illiberality and injustice of the imputations which are so unsparingly cast upon the tribunal, on the alleged score of its supposed cruelties and severity. Thus, in regard of torture and burning, he shows that

Preface

these detestable instruments were, at the periods principally alluded to, no more employed *by it* than they were *then* made use of by all the other civil courts of justice throughout Europe. He shows, moreover, that the accounts of these alleged cruelties are very greatly exaggerated; and that, when any act of great severity did take place, it was only in regard of such criminals as were very notoriously guilty; and that, on all such occasions, the clemency of the priesthood regularly interfered to mitigate the punishment.

In the Third, he presents specimens of the accounts with which travellers—and particularly our English travellers—amuse and feed the credulity of the public on the subject of the Inquisition. For this purpose, he selects the frightful tales related by the pious and learned Rector of Pewsey, the Rev. Mr. Townsend. This interesting traveller, after a residence of two years in Spain, relates—in a clever and well-written work of three volumes—a variety of facts and events relating to the tribunal, which have, no doubt, contributed powerfully to confirm the faith of many an orthodox believer; as well as to terrify the feelings of many a pious lady. The Count, therefore, selects a few of these important instances: and he discusses and criticises them with a considerable share of good humour. He shows that, when strictly analysed and examined, they amount to little else than so many silly tales and cock-and-bull stories.

In the Fourth, he describes some of the benefits which Spain had derived from the interference and influences of the Inquisition. He shows that, whilst other nations have been the theatres of wars, bloodshed, confusion, and every kind of horrors, Spain alone—owing to that tribunal—had, during the course of nearly three centuries, enjoyed an uninterrupted succession of order, union, and tranquillity.

The Fifth Letter is addressed, almost exclusively, to the English, with whose language, history, and literature the Count was intimately acquainted. In it, he shows that the principle of private judgment conducts directly, and inevitably, to a system of complete indifferentism in relation to real Christian faith; secondly, that, notwithstanding all their boasted professions of liberty and toleration, the English are grossly intolerant, and have been always the violent persecutors of the Catholics.

Such is, briefly, the outline of the succeeding *Letters*. The Protestant who reads them—should any read them—however prejudiced or bigoted he may be, will, at all events, own this—that they are the work of a superior mind; of an elegant writer; and of a well-informed politician.

My motive for publishing the *Letters* has not been to defend the Inquisition—much less to vindicate any of its abuses, or alleged severities. I consider persecution, under every form whatsoever, both as uncatholic and unchristian. My motive has been to prove that the imputations which are so unceasingly urged against the Catholic religion under the pretext of the conduct and supposed cruelties of that tribunal, are unfounded and unjust—the dictates of ignorance, and the effusions of malevolence and prejudice.

To the *Letters* I have appended a few notes and illustrations. My motives for doing this have been, in the first place—by exposing the savage character, and the barbarous execution, of our own penal laws—to show the Protestant how little reason he has to insult the Catholic with the reproaches of persecution; and in the next place, from the circumstance of the repeal of the dreadful code, to make the Catholic sensible how much he owes to the happy change of times; and to the justice and humanity of our present enlightened rulers.

Northampton, September, 1838.

ON THE SPANISH INQUISITION

First Letter

Monsieur Le Comte,

I HAVE had the satisfaction of exciting both your interest and your astonishment in the course of our conversations on the subject of the Inquisition. You have, therefore, for your own use and convenience, requested me to commit to writing the different reflections which I have presented to you concerning this celebrated institution. With this request I now most willingly comply: and I will take this opportunity to collect, and place before you, a certain number of observations and authorities which I could not have adduced in the course of a simple conversation. Without any other preface than this, I shall begin my dissertation with the history of the awful tribunal.

I remember having remarked to you, in general terms, that one of the most honourable attestations in favour of the Inquisition is the Official Report itself of that philosophical Cortes, which, in the year 1812, suppressed this tribunal: but which, by the exercise of their brief and arbitrary power, contrived to satisfy nobody but themselves.[1]

If you consider the character and the spirit of this assembly, but particularly of its committee, which drew up the decree of suppression, you cannot but own that any acknowledgment in favour of the Inquisition, coming from such authority, is itself a circumstance which admits of no reasonable reply.

Certain modern unbelievers, the echoes of Protestant ignorance and illiberality, (A) have contended that St. Dominic was the author and founder of the Inquisition: and for this

---

1 *Informe sobre el tribunal de la Inquicision con el projecto de decreto acerca de los tribunales, protectores de la Religion, presentado a las Cortes generales y extraordinarias por la comision de constitucion.* Mundado imprimir. Cadix. 1812.

reason, they have not failed declaiming against him with all the fury of their indignation. Now, the fact is that St. Dominic neither ever exercised any act of an Inquisitor; nor had he anything to do with the Inquisition. The origin of the Inquisition is dated from the Council of Verona, in the year 1184:[2] and the superintendence of it was confided to the order of the Dominicans only in the year 1233, that is, at least twelve years after the death of St. Dominic.

In the twelfth century the heresy of the Manicheans, who in our times are better known under the name of Albigenses, appeared to threaten both the peace of the church and the stability of the state. For the security, therefore, of both, it was deemed necessary to send among them certain ecclesiastical commissioners to inquire after the guilty. These commissioners called themselves *Inquisitors*; and their institution was approved by Innocent the Third, in the year 1204. At first, the Dominicans acted as delegates from the Pope and his legates. As the *Inquisition* was then but an appendage to their *preaching*, they derived from this—their principal function—the name of the *Preaching Friars*, a name which they have always retained. Like all institutions which are destined to produce any great effects, the Inquisition was by no means, in its commencement, the powerful instrument which subsequently it became. These kinds of institutions, all of them, grow and establish themselves, one knows not how. Called in, and introduced by circumstances, opinion, in the first instance, approves of them. Ere long, authority, sensible of the advantages it may derive from them, sanctions them; and models them into form and order. For these reasons, it is not an easy matter to assign the precisely fixed epoch of the Inquisition, which, from feeble beginnings, advanced gradually towards its full dimensions—which is the case with everything that is destined to last. However, this is what may with confidence be asserted—that the *Inquisition*, properly so called, with all its attributes, and in its real character—was never legally established before the year 1233, in virtue of the Bull—"*Ille humani generis*" of Gregory the Ninth, addressed, April the 24th, to the Provincial of Toulouse. While, moreover, it is equally incontestable *that the first Inquisitors opposed no other arms to the growing heresy, save those of prayer, patience, and instruction.* (B)

---

2 Fleuri. *Hist. Eccles.* L. lxxiii. No. liv.

First Letter

Allow me, Sir, to make here just one passing observation—It is this, that it is always wrong and injudicious to confound the character—or if I may so express it—the *primitive*, spirit, of any institution, with the changes and variations which circumstances, and the wants and passions of men, compel it to undergo in the process of time. Of its own nature, the Inquisition is a good, mild, and conservative tribunal. Such, in fact, is the universal, the unvarying, and the indelible character of every ecclesiastical institution. Such, as you cannot but have observed, is the case at Rome: and such, also, you will equally find is the case wherever the church commands. But should the civil power, adopting this institution, think proper for its own security to render it more severe, the Church then, in this case, is no longer responsible for it.

Towards the end of the fifteenth century, the prevalence and power of the Jews were so great in Spain; and Judaism had everywhere spread and fixed its roots so deeply, as absolutely to threaten the destruction, both of the national religion and of the national prosperity. "*The riches of the Jews,*" say the annals of that period, "*their influence, their alliances with the most illustrious families of the monarchy, were circumstances, which rendered them infinitely formidable. They really formed a nation within a nation.*"

In addition to these dangers, resulting from the power and influence of the Jews, there came in, also, to augment them—and to augment them frightfully—the growth and propagation of Muhammadanism. The tree, in Spain, had been shivered and blown down; but its roots still lived. The question, therefore, was to ascertain whether there should still exist such a thing as a Spanish nation; or whether Judaism and Islamism should possess, and divide between themselves, its rich and beautiful provinces—that is, whether superstition, despotism, and barbarity should triumph over the piety, the liberty, and the happiness of mankind. The Jews were, at this time, nearly the masters of Spain: and there existed between them and the Catholic body a mutual, and mortal, hatred. The Cortes, therefore, now demanded the introduction of severe and coercive measures against them. In 1391 they rebelled: and multitudes of them perished. As, however, the danger was every day increasing, Ferdinand, surnamed "the Catholic," conceived that, in order to save Spain, nothing would contribute more effectually than the Inquisition. To this, Isabella at first made strong objection. But, at length, she was induced to consent: and Sixtus IV, in the year 1478, issued out the Bulls of institution.

Permit me, again, my Lord, before I proceed any farther, to suggest to your consideration another important observation: It is this, *that never can any great political disorder—but, above all, any violent attack upon the body of the state—be prevented or repelled, but by the adoption of means alike violent and energetic.* This is one of the most incontestable axioms in the code of politics. In all real and imminent dangers, the rule of Roman prudence, "*Videant Consules, ne respublica detrimentum capiat*" ["let the consuls see to it that the state receive no harm"] is the dictate of enlightened policy. In regard of the methods to be employed, or actually employed, on such occasions, the best are those—I, of course, exclude crime and injustice—the best are those which succeed. If you consider only the severities of Torquemada without calculating the evils which they prevented—you, in this case, cease to reason.

Wherefore, let us constantly bear in mind this fundamental truth—*That the Inquisition, in its origin, was an institution demanded and established by the kings of Spain, under very difficult and extraordinary circumstances.* This is expressly acknowledged by the Committee of the Cortes. (Rep. p. 37). And the reason, which that assembly assigns for its suppression, is simply the consideration that, "*as circumstances are now changed, so the Inquisition is now no longer necessary.*" (R. Ibid).

People have often expressed their surprise at seeing the Inquisitors overload an accused person with a multiplicity of questions, in order to ascertain the fact whether or not, in his genealogy, he retained any portion or drop of Jewish or Muhammadan blood. "What matters it," they say, "to know who was the grandfather, or the great-grandfather, of the accused?" What matters it? It, at that time, mattered greatly: because both of the proscribed races, being still intimately connected and allied with the great families of the state, must necessarily, either have trembled, or have created terror. (R. Ibid. p. 67).

Under these circumstances, it became a concern of prudence to strike and alarm the imagination by constantly holding out the threat of the anathema attached to the suspicion of Judaism, and Muhammadanism. It is a great mistake to suppose that, in order to get rid of a powerful enemy, it suffices always merely to arrest him. You must subdue him; or you have done nothing.

First Letter

With the exception of a small number of enlightened individuals, you hardly ever, in society, meet with a person, who, speaking of the Inquisition, is not impressed with three capital errors—and these so fast riveted to the mind as not to yield to the very plainest demonstrations.

For example, the public everywhere believe that the Inquisition is a purely ecclesiastical tribunal—a notion, which, in the first place, is false. Secondly, they believe that the ecclesiastics, who sit in this tribunal, condemn certain accused criminals to death. This again is false. Thirdly, they believe that the tribunal condemns men for entertaining mere simple opinions. This, too, is another falsehood. (C)

The tribunal, then, of the Inquisition, is purely and completely *Royal*. It is the King alone who appoints the Inquisitor General. And the Inquisitor General, in his turn, nominates the particular Inquisitors, subject to the approval of the King. The constitutional rules and order of the tribunal were drawn up and published, in the year 1484, by Cardinal Torquemada, "*in concert with the King.*" (R. p. 32).

The inferior Inquisitors possessed no power to do anything without the approbation of the Grand Inquisitor: neither could the latter do aught without the concurrence and sanction of the Supreme Council. This Council was not established by any Bull of the Pope; so that in the case of the General Inquisitor's charge becoming vacant, the members of the tribunal proceeded to act alone—not as ecclesiastical, but as *royal* judges. (R. p. 34, 35).

The Inquisitor General, in virtue of the Bulls of the Sovereign Pontiff; and the King, in virtue of his royal prerogatives, constitute the authority which has always regulated the tribunals of the Inquisition. These tribunals are, thus, at once ecclesiastical and royal; so that, on the supposition of one or other of the two powers receding, the action of these tribunals would, in such case, be necessarily suspended. (R. p. 36).

The committee of the Cortes, in their Report, have thought proper to represent the two powers as in a state of equilibrium, in the tribunals of the Inquisition. But, no one, surely, can be the dupe of such misrepresentation—or of the falsehood of this pretended equilibrium. The Inquisition is purely a royal instrument—completely and exclusively under the control of the King; and powerless to do evil, save through the fault of his ministers. If the proceedings in any cause are not regular; or the proofs not clear, the King's Councillors can always—where there is question of capital punishments—at once, and by one word, annul the whole process. Neither religion nor the priesthood have, in such cases, anything at all to do in the concern. If unhappily it do so chance that the accused is punished without being guilty, the fault and the injustice would then be either in the King, whose laws had unjustly ordained the punishment; or else in the magistrates, who unjustly inflicted it. But of this I will cite the proofs hereafter.

You may remark, my Lord, that, among the numberless declamations, which have been published against the Inquisition, you never trace so much as one word respecting this distinctive character of the tribunal—a circumstance, however, which, in justice, all writers on the subject ought essentially to have remarked. Thus, Voltaire, for example, in a hundred passages of his works, describes the tribunal as the instrument exclusively of priestly cruelty, and injustice:

> Ce sanglant tribunal,
> Ce monument affreux du pouvoir monacal,
> Que L'Espagne a reçu; mais, qu'elle même abhorre;
> Qui venge les autels, mais qui les déshonore,
> Qui, tout couvert de sang, de flammes entouré,
> Egorge les mortels avec un fer sacré.
>
> ["This bloody tribunal,
> That frightful monument of monkish power,
> Which Spain has received; but which she herself abhors;
> Which avenges the altars, but dishonours them,
> Which, all covered with blood, encircled by flames,
> Slaughters mortals with a sacred sword."]

Now, this tribunal—although thus frightfully depicted—is, nevertheless, the tribunal of a nation, distinguished for its wisdom, its moderation, and its high sense of honour. It is a tribunal, strictly royal, composed of such members only of the clergy as are remarkable for their learning and their abilities; and who, judging of real crimes, in virtue of the public and pre-existing laws, pronounce their sentence, with a measure of equity and wisdom which perhaps could nowhere be found in any other Court of Justice. They never condemn anyone, however criminal, to death. Hence, then, in what terms can I express the infamy of the base calumniator, who, in the above verses, thus insolently misrepresents an order of men, who, so far from being cruel, are even remarkable for their clemency and moderation. But the truth is, Voltaire had his reasons for hating all authority.

If men were, all of them, wise and well instructed, the absurdities and falsehoods, like the foregoing, would excite only their ridicule and contempt. But unfortunately, such is not the case. The public—ignorant and prejudiced—are easily imposed upon and deceived. And the consequence is that, cheated by the gross misrepresentations of a host of calumniating writers, they look upon the Inquisition as a club of stupid and ferocious monks, who roast men for their own amusement. Nay, it is even true—such is the force of prejudice and ignorance—that the same erroneous and unjust notions prevail even in the minds of a multitude of individuals, who, in other regards, are distinguished for their good sense. You may find them, moreover, in the works, not unfrequently, of the very defenders of sound and virtuous principles. Thus, for example, in the *Journal de L'Empire*, you may read the following strange passage: "*Il est vrai, quoi qu' on en dit, que les Inquisiteurs avoient conservé, jusqu' en 1783, l'habitude, un peu sévère, de bruler solennellement les gens, qui ne croyoient qu' en Dieu. C'etoit là leur tic; mais, hormis ce point, ils étoient de fort bonne composition.*" ["It is true, whatever else may be said of them, that the Inquisitors had maintained, until 1783, the somewhat severe habit of solemnly burning people who did not but believe in God. This was their habit; but, apart from this point, they were of very good character."] (D)

Surely the author of this passage could never have reflected seriously upon what he writes. Where, then—in what nation of the globe—does there exist a tribunal which never condemned anyone to death? Or what crime does any civil tribunal commit which condemns the accused to death in virtue of a law of the state, ordaining such punishment for the crime of which he is proved to have been guilty? And where, again, is the Spanish law which ordains that the Deists shall be put to death? The boldness of such assertion is as impudent an attempt to impose upon the credulity of the public as injustice or bigotry could well have invented.

Amid the numberless errors which the enemies of our religion have propagated; and with too deplorable success, impressed deeply on the minds of the public—I hardly know any that have surprised me more than the supposition and belief that priests are ever permitted to condemn anyone to death. Men may be excused for not knowing the religions *of Fo*, *of Buddha*, or *of Somonocondom*—although still, whoever undertakes to defame even these preposterous systems, ought first, in justice, to understand something at least about them. But for a Christian to be ignorant of the laws of universal Christianity—this, surely, is a disorder which no apology can justify. For what eye has not seen that immense and lucid Orb suspended, for eighteen hundred years, between heaven and earth? Or what ear has not heard that eternal axiom of our religion, that *The Church Abhors Blood?* Who does not know that the priest is even forbidden to be a surgeon, lest his consecrated hands shed the blood of a man—although it be even for his cure? Who does not know that, in many Catholic nations, the priest is dispensed with from appearing as a witness in the trials of life and death? And that even in the countries where such condescendence is not allowed—he is still allowed to enter his protest, *that he only appears, as such, in obedience to the laws, and in order to plead for mercy?* Never does the priest erect the scaffold. He ascends it, only as the martyr or the comforter. He preaches naught but clemency and pity; and in no corner of the globe does he shed any other blood but his own.

"The Church," says Pascal,

> the chaste Spouse of the Son of God, is always, in imitation of this merciful Being, prepared and ready to shed her blood for the sake of others; but not to shed that of others for her own sake. She entertains the most decided horror of bloodshed—proportioned to that particular light which God has communicated to her. She considers men, not simply as men, but as the images of the God whom she adores. She cherishes for each and every individual that holy respect which renders them all venerable in her sight—as having been purchased and redeemed at an infinite price, in order to become, one day, the temples of the Living God. For these reasons it is, that she looks upon the death of an individual, inflicted without an order from God, not only as an act of murder; but as a sacrilege, moreover—depriving her thus of one of her members: because whether the person thus sacrificed be one

of the faithful or not, she still always considers him either as being one of her children; or else, capable of becoming such.

It is very well known that no private individual is permitted to require the death of another. Whence, it became necessary to establish public officers to do this, by the authority of the King—or rather, by that of the Almighty. And hence, again, in order to act as the faithful dispensers of the divine power, in all cases of life and death the magistrates have no liberty of judging and deciding, save by the testimony and the depositions of witnesses—in consequence of which, they can neither, in conscience, pass any sentence but according to the dictate of the law; nor condemn anyone to death but him whom the law condemns. And then, too, if the order of God obliges them to consign the body of the wretched criminal to punishment, the same order of God obliges them, again, to take care of his guilty soul. In all this there is nothing but what is right and completely innocent: "*and still, so much does the Church abhor the shedding of blood, that she declares all those incapacitated for the service of her altars who have ever participated in a sentence of death, although this were attended by all the aforesaid religious circumstances.*"

You cannot, Sir, but admire the beauty, and own the wisdom, of the above theory. Perhaps, however, you may wish, likewise, to know, by experience, the true spirit of the priesthood in relation to this interesting object. Well then, study and consider this, in those countries or places where the *priesthood* once held, or still holds, the sceptre. A series of extraordinary circumstances had formerly established in Germany a multitude of Ecclesiastical Sovereignties. To judge of these, under the heads of clemency and justice, you need only to call to your recollection the old German proverb—"*It is good to live under the crosier.*" Proverbs, which are the fruit of public experience, are testimonies which never deceive us. I therefore appeal to this authority, which is still farther confirmed by the sanction of every man who possesses either memory or judgment. Never under those mild and pacific governments was there any question of persecution; nor of any capital sentence against the spiritual enemies of the reigning powers.

And what, Sir, shall I say of Rome? It is, no doubt, under the government of the Sovereign Pontiffs that the spirit of the priesthood should manifest itself the most unequivocally. Now, it is an incontestable and universally admitted truth that never has this government been reproached with aught but its too great mildness. Nowhere does there exist a more paternal administration; a more impartial distribution of justice; an order of punishment more gentle and humane—a measure of toleration more complete. Rome is, perhaps, the only place in Europe where the Jew is neither humbled nor ill-treated. At all events, it is most certainly the place where he is the happiest—for, Rome has always been proverbially called, "*The Paradise of the Jews.*"

In like manner, consult the voice of history. What government do you anywhere find that has been less severe than that of modern Rome in relation to every kind of anti-religious offences and disorders? Even during those periods which are called "*the ages of ignorance and fanaticism*"—not even then did its spirit or its practice vary. Thus, let me just cite to you the example of Clement IV absolutely *scolding* the King of France—and this King was St. Louis himself—for having made certain laws against blasphemers which that Pontiff thought too severe—intreating him, at the same time, very urgently, in his Bull of July 12th, 1268, to mitigate them. He, moreover, in another Bull of the same date, addressed to the King of Navarre, remarks to this Prince: "*It is by no means advisable to imitate the example of our very beloved Son in Jesus Christ—the Illustrious King of France—in regard of those too rigorous laws which he has published against these kinds of crimes.*"

Voltaire, in some of those moments when his common sense was not obscured by the clouds or fever of irreligion, has, on several occasions, borne very honourable testimony to the Papal government. Thus, in his poem "*De la Loi Naturelle*" he says:

> Marc-Aurèle, et Trajan, mêloient, au champ de Mars,
> Le bonnet du Pontife au bandeau des Césars,
> L'univers, reposant sous leur heureux génie,
> Des guerres de l'école ignoroit la manie.
> Rome, encore aujourd'hui, conservant ces maximes,
> Joint le trône à l'autel par des nœuds légitimes.
> Ses citoyens en paix, sagement gouvernes,
> Ne sont plus conquérans; et sont plus fortunés.

["Aurelius, Trajan, princes of renown,

First Letter

> The pontiff's bonnet wore, and emperor's crown:
> The world depended on their care alone,
> And the schools' vain disputes were then unknown;
> Those legislators, with sage maxims fraught,
> Ne'er for their sacred birds with fury fought.
> On the same principle Rome now holds command,
> The throne and altar by their union stand."][3]

Where such, then, is the evidence of the general character of the Church, why should it anywhere be called in question? Mild, tolerant, charitable, in every nation of the globe—why, or by what magic, does it so chance that she is cruel alone in Spain, a nation eminently distinguished for its high sense of honour, and for the generosity of its subjects?

I must here premise an important observation: It is this—that in the discussion of all questions, be these what they may, there is nothing so essential as to avoid a confusion of ideas. Wherefore, when we speak or reason about the Inquisition, let us always separate and distinguish accurately the conduct of the state from the conduct of the Church. Whatever in this tribunal is rigorous and frightful—but, above all, the punishment of death—all this is purely the concern of the civil government: it is its affair; and it alone is accountable for it. Whereas all the clemency, which is so remarkable in this tribunal, is the act and influence of the Church, which interferes with punishments only in order either to suppress or to mitigate them. Such is its indelible, and never varying, character. Not only is it an error—it is even a crime to maintain or yet to suppose that the *priesthood* can ever pronounce the sentence of death upon anyone.

In the history of France there is a grand event which is not sufficiently noticed. It is that which regards the Templars. These unfortunate beings, whether guilty or not, (this is not here the question) petitioned earnestly to be tried by the tribunal of the Inquisition—"*knowing well*" say their historians, "*that if they could only succeed in obtaining its members for their judges, they should run no risk of being condemned to death.*"

The King of France, however, aware of this, and of the inevitable consequences of this appeal of the Templars, formed now his own determination. He shut himself up, alone, with

---

3 [Translation taken from *The Works of Voltaire, Vol. X: The Dramatic Works Part 1*, tr. William F. Fleming, 1901.]

his Council of State; and at once hastily condemned them to death. This is a fact, which is not, I believe, sufficiently or generally known.

At the earlier periods of the Inquisition, and when the greatest severity was chiefly needed, the Inquisitors in Spain used not to inflict any punishment more rigorous than the confiscation of the criminal's property; and even this was always remitted whenever he thought proper to abjure his errors, within the term, so called, "*of Grace*." (Rep. p. 33). It does not appear quite clear from the instrument thus referred to at what exact period it was that the tribunal of the Inquisition began to pass the sentence of death. This, however, is not material. It suffices to know—what cannot be called in question—that it could only have acquired this right by having become a Royal Institution; and that with the sentences of death the priesthood, from the nature of their character, had not—could not have—anything at all to do.

In our times the matter is no longer an object of incertitude. It is now well known that every important sentence—even the sentence of simple arrest—was decided by the advice of the Supreme Council, without whose authority nothing was, in fact, determined. (R. p. 64). Now, this is a circumstance which pre-supposes and implies both the greatest prudence and the most careful circumspection. But, in short, if it did so happen that the accused was pronounced a heretic—the tribunal, in this case, after having ordered the confiscation of his property, made him over, for the legal punishment, to the secular arm—that is, to the Council of Castile—a body of men than whom nothing in any nation could be more enlightened, more learned, or more impartial. If the proofs alleged against the accused did not appear evident—or if even, though guilty, he did not remain obstinate—the only punishment which then was inflicted on him was simply an act of abjuration, performed in the church, and attended by certain prescribed ceremonies. It is true—all this implied a certain measure of disgrace to the family of the criminal: and to the criminal himself it involved the incapacity of exercising any public employment. (R. p. 65). I am, however, perfectly convinced that, in regard of these latter dispositions, they were but the artifices of clemency, invented for the express purpose of sheltering the greatest criminals. Certain facts, which have come to my own knowledge; and above all the character itself of the tribunal, leave no doubt whatsoever upon my mind in

First Letter

these respects.

The tribunal of the Inquisition is composed of one Supreme head, named the *Grand Inquisitor*, who is always either an archbishop or a bishop; of eight Ecclesiastical Councillors, of whom six are always seculars, and two regulars—one of these invariably a Dominican, in virtue of a privilege granted to the Dominican Order by Philip the Third; the other, a Religious of any other Order, according to the regulation of Charles the Third. The youngest of the Secular Councillors acts the part of an Attorney-General; and in certain cases calls in to his assistance two of the Councillors of Castile. I, however, suppose, at the same time, that they are always called together whenever there is question of any capital punishment. From this plain and simple exposition of facts, you cannot but feel how groundless and fictitious are those two phantoms of Voltaire—as well as of thousands of other ignorant and prejudiced writers—proclaiming the Inquisition, "*a bloody and frightful monument of monkish power.*" There is, surely, nothing very terrific in the circumstance of seeing two humble Religious, united with eleven, or thirteen, judges: whilst, as for the poor insulted Dominicans, to whom the public prejudice attributes all the odium of the Inquisition—your candour will, I am sure, allow it—these men are wholly undeserving of the unjust imputation which is thus cast upon them.

Whoever considers attentively the whole form and order of the tribunal cannot but be compelled to admit that it would be difficult to conceive any possible court of justice, whose composition is better calculated to prevent or to efface even the slenderest suspicion of cruelty—or rather, I will venture to say it—of simple severity. There is no one—provided he but understands the spirit and maxims of the Catholic priesthood—but must be convinced that, in its tribunals, mercy will necessarily hold the sceptre.

And let me here suggest to you, in particular, the following observation—that, independently of the favourable presumptions which arise from the composition alone of the tribunal of the Inquisition—it, moreover, supposes and presents an infinite number of particular mitigations, which all turn out to the advantage of the accused; and which are known only by experience.

But, in order not to dwell any longer upon this part of my subject, I will at once place before you one of the sentences of the Inquisition, of the most severe and rigorous character.

It is one which, without ordering the death of the criminal, (that is impossible) still draws that punishment after it—on the supposition that the guilt be such as the law ordains shall be visited by this infliction. The following, then, is the form and nature of the sentence.

"*We have declared; and do hereby declare, that the accused, N.N., is convicted of being an* APOSTATE *heretic;*[4] *an encourager and concealer of heretics; a false and pretended* CONFESSANT;[5] *and a relapsed impenitent, by which crimes he has incurred the punishments of the greater excommunication and the confiscation of all his goods to the profit of the Royal Chamber and of his Majesty's Attorney-General.*[6] *We, moreover, declare that the accused ought to be left—as we now leave him—to justice, and to the secular arm—intreating these—and very affectionately, and in the best and strongest manner that we can—*CHARGING *them to treat the criminal with kindness and compassion.*"

The Spanish author of "*The Inquisition Unmasked,*" who has furnished me with the above details, pretends, it is true, that the clause, thus recommending mercy, is no other than a mere unavailing formality, and of no service to the criminal. And in order to prove this he cites the words of Van-Espen—according to whom the protestation made by the Tribunal is little else than a kind of external formality—*which, nevertheless, is dear to the Church.*

Now, this objection does not, after all, in any degree weaken the general proposition *that the Inquisition never* ITSELF *condemns any one to death; and that* ON NO OCCASION *will there be found the name of any priest inscribed on any warrant for such*

---

4 The question, therefore, is not of a pure and simple heretic—but of an *apostate* heretic—that is, of a Spanish subject, convicted of having apostatised; and of having given exterior proofs of his apostacy: for, without these, no trial would have taken place.

5 This relates to the crime of *relapse*. For the fact is, the criminal, who confessed his crime, and who said: "*I have sinned; and I repent,*" was always absolved at the tribunal of the Inquisition—an example of clemency, this, such as can nowhere be found in any other Court of Justice. But should the criminal, after this act of mercy, return to his former errors, he, in this case, is declared "*a false and pretended Confessant; and a relapsed Impenitent.*"

6 Thus, the tribunal is purely Royal, notwithstanding the ecclesiastical fiction; and all the fine phrases and declamations against *sacerdotal avidity* come to nothing.

execution.

Where the laws of Spain ordain the punishment of death for such or such a crime, the Courts of Justice cannot, of course, oppose them. Thus, if the Inquisition, after the most diligent investigation, and from the clearest evidence, find the accused guilty of the crimes imputed to him, its judgment then—if it be a case of death, regulated by the laws—will, therefore, be followed by death. But with this the Tribunal itself has nothing at all to do; and it is—and for ever will be—true, that it never condemns anyone, however guilty, to death. The civil power acts, and has the authority to act as it thinks proper. But if, by virtue of the foregoing clause, "*dear to the Church*", its judges condemned any innocent man to death, themselves, in such case, would be the great offending criminals.

Hence, then, that unceasingly repeated expression, calling the Inquisition "*a bloody tribunal*" is not merely groundless, but absurd. There does not—there cannot—exist anywhere a tribunal, but what, unhappily, is sometimes under the necessity of condemning the criminal to death; and which is irreproachable for doing so—provided it but executes the law upon the most positive and clearest evidence—and which even would be justly reproachable if it did not execute the law upon such testimony.[7]

It is, moreover, a fact, that the Inquisition does not itself condemn anyone to the punishment of death, ordained by the dictate of the laws. This is a matter purely, and essentially, civil—be the appearances ever so much against it. And upon this point the Committee itself of the Cortes agrees with the author of "*The Inquisition Unmasked*", whom I have cited already.

"Philip the Second," says the Committee, "'the most absurd of Princes', was the real founder of the Inquisition. It was his refined policy that exalted it to the height of authority to

---

7 There is not a more common, nor a more favourite, expression among Protestant writers—as well as among the Protestant public—than to call all the criminals that are condemned by this tribunal, "*The Victims of the Inquisition.*" They are no more "*victims*" than are all other criminals who are put to death in virtue of a legal sentence. And it is even true that the Inquisition never, but at the last extremity, and after every effort to reclaim the accused criminal, makes him over to the civil power.

which it rose. Our monarchs have always rejected the counsels and suspicions which, at times, have been addressed to them against this tribunal. And their reasons were—because, in every case, they were the absolute masters of naming, suspending, or dismissing the Inquisitors; whilst, at the same time, themselves had nothing to apprehend from the tribunal." (R. p. 69).

From these concessions of the Committee, I think it evident that the tribunal of the Inquisition was completely under the control, not of the priesthood, but of the civil or royal authority. Or if the preceding passage do not convince you of this, I will cite to you another from the same Report, in which the Committee observes that, "in no Papal Bull can it be found that the Supreme Council has the right to decide any cause in the absence of the Grand Inquisitor—but which, however, is constantly done, without the slenderest difficulty." Whence, the Reporter of the Committee concludes, that, "*in these cases, the Councillors act, not as ecclesiastical, but as royal judges.*" (R. p. 35). But, beyond all this, is it not an incontestable fact, that, "*neither at present, nor formerly, could any order of the Inquisition be, I do not say, executed, but so much as published, without the previous consent of the King.*" (R. p. 89).

It was for these reasons that the Kings of Spain have, at all periods, been strongly attached to the Inquisition. Thus, Charles the Fifth, when petitioned by the states of Aragon and Castile to render the proceedings of the Inquisition less severe, replied (for, he was a Prince, who pretty well understood the art of ruling) to their address, in terms the most ambiguous—seeming to grant everything, and yet, in reality, granting nothing. (R. p. 50). Whence, Garnier—an historian, who on this subject is, of all others, the least to be suspected—very candidly allows that "*the Religious Inquisition was nothing more nor less than a Political Institution.*"[8]

It is a fact which merits notice that, in the year 1519, the Aragonese had obtained from Leo the Tenth the complete concession of all their petitions upon this subject—a circumstance which strikingly points out the spirit of the Church and the character of her Pontiffs. However, Charles V opposed the execution of the Papal Bulls; and Leo, in order that he might not disgust the King, issued, in 1520, the Bull, in which he approves of Charles's conduct. (R. p. 52).

---

8 *Hist. de Charlemagne.*

First Letter

I have thus stated to your Lordship the character of the Inquisition. From it, and from the facts which I have cited, you will be convinced how groundless are the notions which the public everywhere entertain of this tribunal; and how unjust the calumnies with which the infidel and the Protestant writers have so bitterly assailed it.[9]

---

9 "In April, 1815," it is stated, in the Madrid Gazette, "Ferdinand VII made a visit to the various prisons of the Inquisition, when—having curiously and carefully examined them—His Excellency, the Inquisitor General, who had accompanied his Majesty, addressed him as follows: "Sire," he said, "your Majesty has now seen these subterraneous prisons; these frightful dungeons; these instruments of torture, against which, in the height of their delirium, the enemies of the throne and the altar declaim so furiously. Have you, then, seen the ministers of the God of peace transformed into so many Neros, and Dioclesians—kindling and fanning the flames of funeral piles, and indulging themselves in every atrocity that cruelty and barbarity can invent? Your Majesty has observed that the prisons are clean and decent; and even commodious; and that the ministers of the Holy Office know how to unite mildness and mercy with justice. May God grant that this visit of your Majesty may have the happy effect of undeceiving men who have abandoned the paths of truth."

Notes and Illustrations.

(A.)

It is to the injustice, principally, and the illiberality of the Protestant writers, that the learned author, the Count De Maistre, in his various works, attributes the hostility of the Infidel writers to the Catholic religion; precisely as he also, in like manner, imputes the infidelity of these men to the principles of Protestantism. The circumstance, indeed, of the injustice and illiberality of the Protestant writers in whatever relates to the Catholic religion is too notorious to be called in question. It is, among them all, "*La fable convenue*"—a matter of course. At least it is so—and peculiarly so—in this country, "*La nation,*" says the Count, "*la plus aisée à tromper; la plus difficile à détromper; et la plus puissant e pour tromper les autres.*" ["The nation easiest to deceive; the most difficult to deceive; and the most powerful in deceiving others."] This opinion is correct—for in no nation are there so many sects and impositions—nowhere so many prejudices and delusions—nowhere greater talents, eloquence, and industry to mislead and deceive the public. Cobbett has asserted in one of his Registers that "*he verily believes that there are more lies in English books than in all the other books in the world put together.*" At all events, I do think this fact true, that, among all the multitude of the antagonists of the Catholic religion in this country, there is not so much as one, who pretending to describe it, does not misrepresent it; or who, affecting to refute its tenets, does not distort, insult, and vilify them. Whence it is, that there is not any one prejudice so deeply burnt into the English mind as the hostility to what is vulgarly denominated "*Popery.*"

There are various causes which, besides the misrepresentations of our religion, account for the general hostility to it. Thus, it is a fact, which may be traced in every age and country, that whenever or wherever men separated themselves from the Parent Church, they at once became its bitterest enemies. Such has uniformly been the case with every heresy and schism that have risen up in the Christian world. But where, added to this, it has, moreover, been the fact that any new sect or heresy has proved triumphant over the Parent institute—despoiling it of its riches; seizing upon its sanctuaries, &c., it, in this case, becomes also the obvious but unhappy interest of such sect or heresy, by every artifice of policy, and by every instrument of violence, to retain the unhallowed usurpation; and to depress and persecute the plundered Church. This is the very instinct, and first dictate, of injustice. Accordingly, describing the conduct of this country in relation to the Catholic religion, the eloquent and patriotic Parnell, in his *Historical Apology*, says: "*To keep alive the prejudices of the public, the government employed all its long chain of influence and activity. It organised every exertion in reviving, inventing, and circulating every libel and slander; every pitiful jealousy; every sordid suggestion; every fierce defiance against the doctrines, opinions, character, and persons of the Catholics.*" Such as these, no doubt, are the surest means of retaining power; and of keeping possession of what the violence of injustice had acquired. But, in fact, it is true that the very name itself of "Protestant,"—a name not denoting any religion whatsoever—for the Atheist is just as much a Protestant as is the believer in the Thirty-nine Articles. This name itself is a name of rancour and hostility.

It is owing, therefore, to the above, and many such like causes, that there exists in this country a spirit of ill-will and bigotry towards the Parent Church, such as is now unknown in every other Protestant state. Gibbon, indeed, asserts that "*the English are the most credulous and fanatic of any nation in Europe.*" At all events, this is certain, that in no other nation in Europe are there employed so many means and instruments—so much industry and artifice—so many falsehoods, insults, and invectives, to poison, inflame, and mislead the public mind in relation to the Catholic religion, as have always been, and are still made use of in this pretendedly liberal and enlightened country. It is, indeed, fortunate for us that the men who now daily write, and speak, and preach, and inveigh against us, have not also the power to do more. I doubt much, whether words alone would satisfy them; and whether they would not bring back those good olden days, when "*the persecution of Catholics*," as Hume relates, "was called THE GOLDEN REINS OF DISCIPLINE."

(B.)—*The Doctrines of the Albigenses.*

Whoever is acquainted with the doctrines and conduct of the Albigenses, will, if candid, allow that the former were so impious and detestable, the latter so violent and seditious, as not only to have justly awakened the vigilance of the states in which they prevailed; but, moreover, to have called down upon them the just severities of the law. Their doctrines, borrowed, many of them, from those of Mani, were such as follow. They believed, like the Manicheans, in two principles or creators—the one good, the other bad; in two Christs, the one good, who had not, as yet, appeared in the world; the other bad, who had appeared in a fantastic body, and who had died, and risen up again, only in appearance. They denied the resurrection of the body; condemned all the sacraments; rejected matrimony; and believed the procreation of children to be a crime. To these and other profane opinions were added the most decided hatred of the hierarchy, and their endeavours by violence and the grossest insults to overturn it, declaiming loudly and forever against the power and riches of the clergy. Their morals, corresponding with their doctrines, were in the highest degree infamous and abominable: whence, also, they received those detestable appellations expressive of their disorders—"Pifres, Patarins, Poplicolins, Cathari, &c."

It was in consequence, more or less, of the aforesaid doctrines, but chiefly from the violence and excesses of their conduct, that they, at length, drew down upon themselves the severities of that crusade, which has furnished a multitude of the Protestant writers, and their copyists, the Incrédules, with such ample room, and with such delightful materials for insult and declamation. I do not indeed pretend to say that the punishments, sometimes inflicted by Simon De Montfort, did not exceed the measure both of mercy and justice. Such probably was the fact. But then they were provoked by the grossest profanations of religion; by the greatest excesses and disorders; and by the most savage cruelties exercised upon the Catholics.[10]

It is a circumstance, also, which should be remarked—that,

---

10 *"Certain writers,"* says Mosheim, *"who have accustomed themselves to entertain a high idea of the sanctity of all those, who, in the Middle Ages, separated themselves from the Church of Rome, suspect the Inquisitors of having attributed falsely impious doctrines to the Albigenses. But this suspicion is entirely groundless. Their shocking violation of decency was a consequence of their pernicious system. They looked upon decency and modest, as marks of inward corruption. Certain enthusiasts amongst them maintained that the believer could not sin let his be ever so horrible or atrocious."*—Eccl. Hist., vol. iii.

for forty years before Montfort's Crusade, every method had been employed to correct the errors and to appease the disorders of the deluded fanatics—instruction, mildness, &c. In 1147 St. Bernard went amongst them, armed only "with the sword of the Spirit—the word of God"—and the virtues and sanctity of his life. In like manner, Voltaire himself observes—St. Dominic went, also, amongst them, carrying with him no other than the same gentle and persuasive influences. *"Saint Dominique,"* he says, *"qui avoit accompagné L'Eveque D'Osma—trés homme de bien—à Toulouse, donna, avec lui, l'example, d'une vie apostolique; et parut souhaiter, qu'on n'employa jamais d'autres armes que la persuasion, et la bonne vie."* ["St. Dominic, who had accompanied the Bishop of Osma, a good man, to Toulouse, furnished, with him, the example of an apostolic life; and seemed to wish that no weapons should ever be employed other than persuasion and the good life."]—Hist. Gen.

It was, in fact, only when all these and such like expedients had proved unavailing, that recourse was had to the measures of severity and repression. In 1179, the Council of Lateran, alleging its reasons for sanctioning these, remarked—*"They,"* (the insurgent fanatics) *"respect neither the churches nor the monasteries. They spare neither orphans, age, nor sex. They plunder and lay waste everything when we exhort the faithful courageously to oppose their ravages."* Such as these were the causes, and such the motives, of the Crusade undertaken against the Albigenses. And where, in fact, is the nation that, even now, under similar provocations and excesses as the above, would not adopt severe and powerful measures to repress them? If the reader will only recall the conduct of this Protestant country towards Catholic Ireland, he may trace in this, and in the savage cruelties exercised upon its Catholic subjects—I do not say, reasons to justify the cruelties of Montfort—no reasons can justify cruelty—but, reasons to silence much of the severity and inconsistency of their reproaches against him.[11]

---

11 It should seem a somewhat singular fact that, considering the doctrines and the conduct of the Albigenses, our English Protestant divines, many of them—such as Fulke, Sparke, Bulkley, &c., and even still, several modern ones—lay claim to these fanatics as the early ancestors of their Church. It is true, they were Protestants; but so also were all and every one of the impure, profane, and impious sects

Maistre

(C.)—*The Inquisition, a Political Institution.*

"*L'Inquisition,*" says M. Guizot—there can be no better authority—"*fut, d'abord, plus politique, que religieuse; et destinée à maintenir l'Ordre, plus tôt quà défendre la foi.*" ["The Inquisition was, at first, more political than religious; and designed to maintain order rather than to defend the faith."]—(Hist. Mod., Lect. 11.) Such, certainly, was the fact. The Inquisition

that, at every period since the dawn of Christianity, separated themselves from the Catholic Church. All these were Protestant. Jewell, indeed, speaking of the Albigenses, says of them: "*They are none of ours.*" However, if other Protestants are fond of the genealogy, we greet them as welcome to it.

Almost equally singular it is in the eyes of the Catholic, that our Protestant writers should claim, as another link in the chain of their ancestry, the cognate sect—sprung principally from the former—of the Lollards. And yet such also is the fact. Speaking of these heretics, Southey—a not incompetent judge—says of them: "*Undoubtedly, the Lollards were highly dangerous. The greater number of them were eager for havoc; and held opinions incompatible with the peace of society. They would have stripped the churches; destroyed the monasteries; confiscated the church lands; and proclaimed the principle that the saints should possess the earth. The public safety required that such opinions should be repressed, founded, as they were, upon gross error.*"—Book of the Church. Accordingly, in order to suppress these enthusiasts, it was the practice in this country, until the reign of the Second Charles, to oblige all sheriffs of counties to take the following oath: "*You shall do all your pain and diligence to destroy, and make cease, all manner of heresies commonly called Lollaries within your bailiwick.*" Reflecting upon this oath, D'Israeli, from whom I have cited it, remarks: "*The Lollards were the most ancient of Protestants, and had practised Luther's sentiments. It was, in fact, condemning the established religion of the country.*"—(Curiosities of Literature.)—Hence, then, that our present defenders of the Established Church should still cling to these men as their religious ancestors, is rather a matter of surprise. However, so it is: They feel, and own, the necessity of an ancestry, *somewhere*; and as they can trace this nowhere but through the ignominious links of the Albigenses and the Lollards, so they are reduced to adopt—and as I have said, they are welcome to it, the strange and singular genealogy. "*But such,*" says Dr. Heylin, "*is the humour of some men, as to call every separation from the Church of Rome the* Gospel.."—Animadversions on Fuller.

was established and preserved as a political instrument, in the hands of governments, to aid the police and to repress disorder, much more than as a spiritual engine in the hands of the clergy to suppress heresy or to punish heretics. Thus, it was nowhere established but at the solicitation of princes—nowhere acted, or exercised any power, but under the authority, and by the direction, of princes. The Popes, save in their own dominions—never erected it in any kingdom, although at the request of certain princes, they were induced to sanction its introduction. But they even sometimes did this with reluctance. It is by no means—as the Protestants assert it is—an institution invented, and exclusively created, by the artifices and the authority of the Popes. This is one of the numberless falsehoods maintained by our Protestant writers, in order to render our religion odious.

(D.)—*Exaggerated Accounts of the Inquisition.*

There is no learned person—provided that he be not deeply prejudiced—but will own that the imputations so often cast upon the tribunal of the Inquisition by the Protestant writers are very grossly exaggerated, and for the most part the fictions of bigotry and the inventions of ill-will. Thus, Voltaire himself, Montesquieu, Bourgoing, and many others who have inveighed against the tribunal, still candidly allow that its enemies have attributed to it a multitude of cruelties and excesses of which it is wholly guiltless. Voltaire even reproaches these men with having forged a number of false tales and doubtful facts for the express purpose of inflaming the public mind and of rendering the institution hateful.

In the Papal dominions, for example, the Inquisition is the most lenient of courts—more lenient far, than any of our ecclesiastical courts in this country. During the course of upwards of a century it has never, on any occasion, nor for any crime, condemned one single criminal to death. Neither, indeed, did the Popes, in the establishment of this tribunal, nor in the order and forms of its proceedings, ever adopt the plans and measures of the monk Torquemada.

Even in Spain itself, where the severity of the institution was the most awful—even there the infliction of the penalty of death was, comparatively speaking, but of rare occurrence. Thus, the inveterate Limborch, presenting a long list of criminals, during a long length of period, admits that out of all these, only fifteen men and four women—alas, far too great a number—were executed. But then, they were executed for the same crimes—sacrilege, gross profanations, treason, witchcraft, &c.—for which, during the Middle Ages, they would have been equally put to death in this country, or in any other country of Europe. And then, too, these executions were ordained, not by the spiritual authority, but by the civil power of the Tribunal.

After all, be all this as it may—it is still true that neither the institution of the Inquisition nor its punishments have anything to do either with any article of Catholic Faith, nor with any point of Catholic discipline. It has always been rejected by many Catholic states and nations, and these too, eminently Catholic—England, Ireland, Scotland, Germany, Naples—whilst, in France and Venice, it could never obtain any permanent establishment. It was even, in many states and places, viewed with just as much aversion by the Catholic as now it is reprobated by the Protestant. At present, I am convinced that there is no English Catholic but what rejoices at its suppression.

At the same time, I believe this—that, if the disciples of the modern school of Philosophism—aye, and a certain portion of our English Protestants—the men who inveigh so fiercely against persecution—if these had the power to do all they wish in relation to the Catholic religion—they would establish an Inquisition against it even more tyrannical than that of Spain. For, only look at the conduct of the former whilst they reigned triumphant during the French Revolution. They then not only persecuted, profaned, and destroyed as much as they could do it, everything Catholic, but they murdered, with savage cruelty, whole hecatombs of its priesthood. Or look equally at the conduct of these men while they recently domineered, or now domineer, in Spain. Like the French Revolutionists, they have not only again persecuted, defiled, and insulted everything connected with religion, but they have sacrificed, also, thousands of its unoffending Clergy. The greatest of persecutors have been the very men who have the most loudly condemned persecution.

The Second Letter

Monsieur Le Comte,

AFTER the supposition that the Inquisition is a purely ecclesiastical tribunal, and that priests can condemn men to death—after this, there needed but one other supposition to complete the absurd phantom of malevolent ignorance—namely, that the Inquisition condemned men for their simple opinions; and that a Jew, for example, was burnt for no other offence than for being purely and simply a Jew. This, indeed, is an assertion which has been so often repeated that multitudes actually believe the preposterous tale.

Among the least excusable calumniators of the insulted Institution, I regret, and am surprised, to find so distinguished a character as Montesquieu. But so it is: we unfortunately see this great writer, with the boldest intrepidity, pouring out the most virulent language against it, on the occasion of a pretended remonstrance of a pretended Jewess. He even makes this the subject of a chapter in his "*Esprit des Loix.*"

Now, the fact is, that the very idea of burning a young, innocent, girl—and this, too, in one of the grand capitals of Europe, for no other offence than that of believing in her own religion, there is, in this, something too horrible to be conceived. The reality of such act would form a national crime, sufficient to call down the deepest disgrace upon a nation—nay, perhaps, even upon a century. But happily, the whole tale is a pitiful calumny—disgraceful only to the writer whose malignant ingenuity invented it.

How long, then, has it been allowed to calumniate nations, and to insult the institutions which they have thought proper to establish among themselves? Or where is the decency, or the justice, of attributing to these institutions acts of the most atrocious tyranny? And to do this, moreover, not only without the sanction of any testimony or proof, but in face of the most notorious evidences to the contrary. In Spain—and in Portugal equally—as in fact it is the case everywhere, no one is ever molested who keeps himself quiet. As for the imprudent enthusiast who dogmatises and disturbs the public order of things—he, if checked in his career, has no one to complain of but himself. There is nowhere, in any nation, a well-regulated government, but what imposes restraints, or some punishment or other, upon the daring attempts to overturn religion. No one has any right to demand of the kings of Spain why, or for what reasons, they have thought proper to ordain such and such punishments for such and such offences. They knew best what were the wants and the interests of the nation. They knew the character of their enemies; and they restrained them in the way which they judged most prudent. The grand, and only, question, and this, too, incontestable, is this—that, in regard of the offences of which I am speaking, no one is ever punished, but in virtue of a universal and well-known law—according to established and invariable forms of justice—and by lawfully constituted judges, deriving their whole authority from the king, and acting completely under his control. Under these circumstances, then, how ill-founded are all the declamations against the tribunal of the Inquisition; and how little reason has any Spaniard to complain! It is true—*man* justly dislikes to be judged by *man*: because, knowing himself, he knows also of what *man* is capable when once he is either blinded by his passions or pushed on by prejudice. But where there is question of *law*—to this, men ought to be submissive—they ought not to attempt to disturb the public peace. Reason and the instincts of nature admit no better rule in these points than the general, enlightened, and disinterested will of a *legislature*, substituted everywhere in place of the particular, ignorant, and partial will of *man*.

If, therefore, the laws of Spain, composed and ordained for the peace and security of the whole nation—if these inflict the punishments of exile, imprisonment, or even death itself against the declared and public enemies of religion—in this case, neither should anyone excuse the criminal who has thus called down the punishment upon himself—neither should the criminal himself complain—seeing that he possessed the most simple means of avoiding it—*that of holding his tongue*.

In regard of the Jews in particular, everyone knows—or should know—that the Inquisition does not, in reality, punish any of these, save such as *relapse*—that is, such as, having solemnly adopted the Christian religion, return again to Judaism. The laws are, indeed, more or less severe against these, as well as against the preachers of Judaism. But then, the remedy was easy—the Christian, or the converted Jew, who chose again to Judaise, were always at full liberty to quit the country. They knew—as did, also, the Jew who undertook to seduce the Christian—they knew to what they exposed themselves by remaining. No individual has any right to complain of a law which is equally made for all.

Men loudly declaim against the *tortures* employed in the tribunals of the Inquisition; and above all against the punishment of *burning*, inflicted for the crimes against religion. All the thunders of eloquence and indignation, particularly among the French Infidel writers, are directed against these alleged atrocities. The fury of their declamation gives a pathos to their philosophy. However, this vanishes at once, if once the subject be but calmly considered according to the rules of sober and calculating logic.

The Inquisitors, it is true, did ordain the infliction of *torture* for certain crimes against religion. But then, they did it in virtue of the laws of Spain, and because it was prescribed by all the tribunals of that nation. It was a punishment adopted anciently by the laws of Greece and Rome; insomuch that Athens, the school of liberty, ordained it, even in regard of its own free citizens. Among modern nations, all these have employed it in order to discover the truth. I am not going to examine how far all this was either wise or unwise; or whether, in former times, there was not as much reason to employ the instrument of torture as now, in these days, there is every reason to suppress it. Be all this as it may, the case is that, since this punishment was no more attributable to the Inquisition than to every other tribunal, so it is unjust to reproach it alone with imputation of cruelty. Let the eloquence or the virulence of Protestant animosity describe all the horrors, or depict, in every hateful colour, the real or imaginary torments inflicted by the judges of the Inquisition. All this, in fact, matters little. The blame or the odium rests, not with the Institution itself, but with the policy of the princes who established it. (A)

And let me, my Lord, just remark here—that, according to the report of the committee of the Cortes, not only the Inquisitors themselves were obliged to attend at the infliction of the torture, but the bishop, also, was ordered to assist at the awful ceremony—although his place was usually supplied by his delegate. (R. p. 63). Now all this presupposes and implies, in this act of rigour, not only a great deal of attention, but all the charity that is allowed to judges.

And not only this—but, as every decree of any moment, even that of a simple arrest could on no occasion be executed without the previous approbation of the supreme council—so it is also certain that the preliminary sentence ordaining the application of torture was subject to the same formality. Under these circumstances, it cannot but be owned that this punishment was accompanied in the tribunals of the Inquisition with every precaution that the nature of things admitted.

Should the king of Spain think proper to abolish the punishment of torture in his dominions, as has been done in France, England, Sardinia, &c., he would, no doubt, act wisely; and the very first to applaud his conduct would be the Inquisitors themselves. But it is unjust and unreasonable to reproach them with a practice which, until lately, had always and everywhere prevailed.[1]

In regard to the punishment of *burning*, this, again, however horrible, was still a universal practice. Without referring to the Roman laws which sanctioned it, we find that all nations pronounced it against such great crimes as violated the most sacred laws of religion. Thus, throughout Europe, it was the custom to burn for sacrilege, parricide, and high treason. This latter crime was—according to the principles of criminal jurisprudence then adopted—divided into two parts, *divine and human* high treason. Every great and enormous crime against religion was considered as an act of high treason against God, which, therefore, could not be less severely punished than the offence of high treason against man. And hence the custom of burning heresiarchs and obstinate heretics. The fact is that in all ages there are certain general notions and ideas which possess and draw men after them; and whose wisdom, or want of wisdom, is never so much as

---

[1] I was conversing some time ago with two distinguished Spanish noblemen, whose situation in society afforded them the means of being fully acquainted with the proceedings of the Inquisition. When I came to speak to them about the torture, they both expressly declared to me that they had never heard so much as one word respecting the punishment of torture in any tribunal of the Inquisition. This, at all events, implies either that the use of this instrument was abolished, or that its application was extremely rare.

The Second Letter

called in question. The reproach, in such cases, should be cast, not upon any individual, but upon the times, and upon mankind in general. (B)

I will not enter—lest I should seem to quit my subject—upon the great question of crimes and punishments. I will not examine whether the punishment of death be just and useful or not; or whether it be wise to increase the severity of punishments according to the atrocity of crimes; and what ought to be the limits of this awful and terrific right. These are, all of them, questions foreign to that which I am now discussing. To acquit the Inquisition from peculiar reproach or censure, this alone is here sufficient—that its tribunals judged and decided like all other tribunals everywhere; that they condemned none to death, except such as were notoriously guilty; and that they never acted, but as the authorised instruments of the lawful and written will of the Sovereign.

It is however my opinion that the heresiarch, and the propagators of impiety, ought very properly to be ranked in the class of great criminals. What deceives us in these points is the unfortunate circumstance of our judging in these matters under the influence of that indifference which, in these times, pervades everything relating to religion—whereas we ought to take as the rule and measure of our judgment the gone-by zeal of olden days—which men, if they like, may call "*fanaticism*"—the word making no difference in the thing. The modern Sophist, seated at his ease in his cabinet, cares not one jot whether the doctrines of Luther were the cause of the thirty years' frightful war or not. But the legislators of ancient days, knowing well the consequences and miseries which the propagation of heresy is calculated to produce, and has produced, in society—shaking its very foundations and deluging its walks, not unfrequently, with blood—knowing this, they deemed it an act of prudence to punish the crime with severity and rigour.

It is true, there is no longer, now, any reason for entertaining the same alarms. And yet, when we reflect that the Inquisition, by its restrictions and authority, would have prevented the French Revolution—it is hard to say whether the Sovereign, who, wholly and without reserve, gave up this instrument, would not, in reality, be doing an injury to humanity.

The Abbé De Vayrac is the first French writer that I know who has spoken with consistency and wisdom on the subject of the Inquisition.[2] But, even at that period—in 1731—he despaired, amid the clamours of ignorance and prejudice, of making any favourable impressions in its regard. "I am convinced," he says, "that if the men who declaim so loudly against the Inquisition considered only the characters of the persons who compose it, they would speak of it very differently from what they do. But what is the most to be lamented is the fact that—such are the public prejudices—I do not entertain the slenderest hope of engaging my fellow-countrymen to believe that the virtues which particularly characterise the Inquisitors are circumspection, wisdom, justice, and integrity. The man who is punished or reprimanded by this tribunal must be either a great criminal or a very weak personage."

In fact, whoever candidly considers the quality of its judges cannot but allow all this. In the first place, nothing can be more upright, more learned, or more incorruptible than the Grand tribunals of Spain. And then, if to this general character we add that of the Catholic priesthood, it is impossible—even without any appeal to experience—not to feel, and be convinced, that nothing in the universe can really be more calm and gentle—more impartial and humane—than the tribunal of the Inquisition. (C).

In this tribunal—which is established, indeed, to strike and alarm the imagination—and which, therefore, in order to produce the designed effect, ought necessarily to be surrounded with certain severe and mysterious forms—in this tribunal, nevertheless, the religious principle preserves always its leading and unextinguishable character. Even amid the terrors or threats of punishment it is still merciful and mild. It is because the priesthood forms a portion of this tribunal that it ought not—does not—resemble any other tribunal. In reality, the very device of its banners—"*Misericordia, et Justitia*" ["Mercy and Justice"]—is such as is unknown to any other tribunal of the Universe. Elsewhere, in every country, *justice alone* is the appendage, and prerogative, of their tribunals. Mercy is the *exclusive* attribute, and property, of the *Sovereign*. The judges would even be deemed rebels, did they presume, *of themselves*, to grant pardons—for this would be arrogating the rights and privileges of the Sovereignty. But, let only the priesthood be called in; and take place among the

2 *Voyage D'Espagne, et D'Italie.*

judges—they will do this upon the express condition alone that the Sovereignty shall concede to them their great prerogative—*Mercy*. *Mercy*, therefore, is thus seated along with Justice: and even takes the precedence of it. The accused criminal is at liberty, before this tribunal, to confess his fault; to ask pardon for having committed it; and to submit to certain religious expiations. This done—behold, at once, his *crime* is changed into a *sin*, and his punishment into an easy and simple penance. He fasts, prays, and mortifies himself. Instead of being dragged to punishment, he recites psalms; goes to confession; and hears mass. Thus prepared and exercised— he is absolved, and restored to his family and to society. If the crime be of a very heinous character; and the criminal continue obstinate—if he must be condemned to death, the *priest*—in this case, retires; and he appears upon the scaffold only to console the unhappy victim.

It is a singular circumstance that this distinctive character of the Inquisition has been solemnly acknowledged by one of the ci-devant Ministers of the French Republic—Mons. Bourgoing, in his *"Nouveau Voyage en Espagne."* And it is hardly less singular to observe the manner in which one of the journalists of that period gives an account of the above writer's work. Take, for example, the following extract.

"Where," says the journalist,

> is the tribunal in Europe, save that of the Inquisition, that acquits the criminal, provided only that he repents, and confesses his repentance? Where is the individual who, maintaining doctrines, subversive both of faith and morality; and proclaiming principles, destructive of peace and social order—where is the individual who, notwithstanding these offences, had not been twice admonished of his guilt by the members of the Inquisition before they proceeded to any farther act against him? If, in spite of their advice, he still persists in his irreligious conduct, he is, in this case, arrested. If he repent, he is set at liberty. Mons. Bourgoing, whose religious opinions are anything but favourable to religion, speaking of the Holy Office, says: *'I will own it, in order to pay that homage which is due to truth, that the Inquisition might be cited, in these days, as the model of equity.'* This is a singular concession. But the fact is—M.

> Bourgoing saw nothing in the tribunal of the Inquisition, save what it really is, the Instrument of the laws for the preservation of peace and order. (D).

In regard of those cruel and frightful forms, so often reproached and imputed to this tribunal—it is my misfortune to give little or no credit to them. At all events, I should like to be upon the spot, in order to judge of them properly. Be the case, however, what it may—if the revolution, which has, of late years, taken place in the habits and opinions of the public, requires certain mitigations in these points, it is in the power of the monarch to ordain them; and to such alteration the Inquisitors would lend themselves most willingly. We know this well—nothing human can be perfect: and there is no institution but what is attended by some abuse or other. You will, I think, do me the justice to believe that no man is less disposed than myself to justify any useless severities. The religious Inquisition of Spain was, in my opinion, not unlike the public Inquisition of Venice, which reigned over the imaginations of the people by the display of certain terrors, composed of little or nothing else than of mere fantastic forms and delusions; and which had the happy effect of maintaining order without shedding one single drop of blood.

It is false, moreover, even in regard of Portugal, that any, however slender an accusation, is looked upon as a sufficient reason for casting an accused person into prison—as it is just equally false that they deny him the heads and motives of the accusations alleged against him, or the knowledge of his accusers—false, again, that they refuse to allow him proper defenders to plead his cause; or that the accusers, who have calumniated him, remain unpunished. I know, indeed, that in Spain the defenders of the accused prisoners had the freest and most confidential access to them; and that even the judges themselves took particular care to inquire and ascertain whether or not these men had done their duty in this regard. Again, in relation to Portugal, it is a fact that the tribunal of its Inquisition never pronounces any sentence respecting the temporal punishment. It simply declares that the criminal is guilty of the crimes imputed to him. It then leaves it to the civil judges to decide what punishments they may think proper to inflict—precisely in the same way as it is done in Spain. As for all confiscations, these all go to the profit of

The Second Letter

the King. The Diocesan Bishops have also the right to take cognisance of any crime, along with the Inquisitors of the tribunal.

Besides all this, I ought, still farther, to observe to you that, in regard to the more or less severe forms of justice, there has never existed anywhere so much as one enlightened nation which, from time to time—and for great and urgent motives—has not instituted certain extraordinary tribunals, divested, almost wholly, of the usual forms of justice. Thus, I will cite to you, as an example, the ancient Prévôtal order of justice of the French. It was the will, or whim, of the Kings of France, that all the great public roads should be everywhere completely safe for travellers. Every traveller was placed directly under their special protection; and the slenderest attempt upon his person or his safety was looked upon as a kind of high treason, which the law punished with the utmost severity, and with the rapidity of lightning. The poor wretch who had robbed a traveller upon the high road, although it was but of a few livres, was seized by the maréchaussée; delivered over to be judged by the Grand Prévôt and two assessors; and in the course of twenty-four hours, broken alive upon the rack; and all this, too, under the eyes of the parliament, which never interfered, because not allowed to do so, in the business.

It is, no doubt, true that this jurisprudence was severe. But then, it was completely at the option of every Frenchman whether or not to rob upon the high roads. The will of the King was that the public should travel upon them in perfect security, and even sleep upon them with impunity. Men have each their own peculiar notions and ideas.

From what I have already said, you cannot, my Lord, but be sensible how many errors and injustices our modern Sophists have placed to the account of the Inquisition. They represent it as a tribunal purely Ecclesiastical, whereas I have shown you, by the most incontestable authorities, that it is nothing of the nature. They boldly assert that the priests in this institution condemn men to death; and this, too, even for simple opinions. And I have convinced you that this is false. They maintain that the Inquisition is the artful invention of the Popes: whereas, referring to history, you have seen that the institution was conceded by the Popes only at the urgent solicitation of Sovereigns; and often with much reluctance—at least in relation to those inflictions which appeared to them too severe. They have contended that the Inquisition enslaves the human mind, and that the writers of Spain all disappeared the instant it was introduced. Whereas, what is the fact? The brightest age of Spanish literature is the very age of Philip the Second—the prince most loudly accused of being the great promoter of the Inquisition: whilst, moreover, it is likewise true that the writers who have principally distinguished Spain all printed and published their works with the express permission of the Holy Office. Mathematics, astronomy, chemistry—all the natural sciences—philology, history, antiquity, &c.—all these are fields in which the human mind may range without control; and without any the slenderest opposition of the Right Reverend Father—the Grand Inquisitor. It surely is not enslaving the human mind merely to ordain and require that a set of profane and impious writers shall not insult religion and revile the dogmas of the state.

The Second Letter

Notes and Illustrations.

(A.)—The Use of Torture.

THE instruments and modes of torture, long employed in this country, and inflicted upon the Catholics, were little inferior in point of cruelty—if at all inferior—to those which the enemies of the Inquisition have imputed to that tribunal. The following were some of them, as described by Mr. Butler, and recently by Mr. Jardine.

The Ordinary Rack. By this, the limbs of the accused were stretched by levers to a length too shocking to mention—beyond the natural measure of the frame.

The Hoop, called *The Scavenger's Daughter*. By this, the body was placed and bent together till the head and the feet met.

The Iron Gauntlet—A screw, which squeezed the hands until the bones were completely crushed.

The Needles, which were thrust under the nails of the accused.

The Little Ease. This was a hole so small that the person confined in it could neither stand, sit, nor lie down straight.

The Dungeon of Rats. "This horrible dungeon," says Mr. Jardine,

> was a cell below high-water mark, and totally dark: and as the tide flowed, innumerable rats which infest the muddy banks of the Thames were driven through the orifices of the walls into the dungeon. Instances are related where the flesh has been torn from the arms and legs of prisoners, during sleep, by the well-known voracity of these animals.

The Denial, and Long Privation, of Food. "Antony Wood," again says Mr. Jardine, "relates that Brian, a person of good education, was specially punished for two whole days and nights by famine, by which he was reduced to such extremities that he eat the clay out of the walls of his prison, and drank the droppings of the roof." The aforesaid Brian was a priest who, besides being thus tormented by famine, was moreover tortured by *needles*, cruelly racked, and as cruelly put to death.

Besides the above modes of torture, there were others of a

more gentle nature. Thus, Mr. Jardine says: "The *gentler method* of torture was that of *tying the thumbs together* and suspending the accused by them to a beam. This," he adds, "was employed by James against Owen, the servant of Garnet."

Such, then, as the above, were some of the various instruments and modes of torture which, during several succeeding reigns, used constantly to be employed against the Catholics, but above all against the Catholic priesthood. "It is perfectly well known," says Mr. Jardine, "to the student of history that the use of torture was lavishly employed under the reigns of the Tudors.[3] "But," he adds, "in the long catalogue of the cases of torture which occurred in the reign of a sovereign whom Protestant historians delight to honour, you will not fail to observe that many instances, and those the most prominent for refinement of cruelty, unquestionably and avowedly arose from Protestant persecution." And then, too, as Mr. Butler remarks, what adds to the cruelty and injustice of the aforesaid inflictions is the circumstance that they were usually employed without any legal proof whatsoever of any guilt or offence in the accused; and without so much as any evidence adduced or offered to criminate them.

(B.)—*English Laws, and Practice, of Burning.*

It was only yesterday—the 9th of George II—that the punishment of burning for witchcraft, conjuration, enchantment and sorcery was done away. Since the time of the Eighth Henry until the above period, the laws of this kingdom against the aforesaid offences were as absurdly cruel as they were, often, very cruelly executed. "The civil law," says Blackstone,

---

3 The same author, though himself a Protestant, honestly remarks that though the rack was employed in the reign of Mary, there is no record of its having been used towards any of those implicated in Wyat's plot, nor towards any of the persecuted Protestants—"a circumstance," the Edinburgh Reviewers observe, "we should hardly have expected to find, inasmuch as the prosecution of the spiritual offence was left to the ordinary Ecclesiastical Courts, aided by Bonner and his Commission. "Neither," adds Mr. Jardine, "is there any proof in the Records of Mary's reign of any torture employed towards heretics or concealers of heretics."—*On the Use of Torture.*

not only punishes with death the sorcerers, but also those who consult them—imitating, in the former, the express law of God—'Thou shalt not suffer a witch to live.' Our own laws have been equally penal—ranking this crime in the same class with heresy and condemning both to the flames.

By a statute of James the First, all persons invoking any evil spirit, or consulting, covenanting with, entertaining, employing, feeding, or rewarding any evil spirit, or taking up dead bodies from their graves to be used in any witchcraft, sorcery, charm, or enchantment; or killing, or hurting, any person by such infernal arts, should be guilty of felony, without benefit of clergy; and suffer death.

"These acts," continues Blackstone,

besides several others, equally cruel and absurd, continued in force till lately, to the terror of all ancient females in the kingdom, and many poor wretches were sacrificed thereby, to the prejudice of their neighbours and their own illusions.

The statute *De Heretico Comburendo* ordained that the Diocesan alone, without the intervention of a synod, might convict of heretical tenets; and unless the convict abjured his opinions; or if after abjuration, he relapsed, the sheriff was bound, *ex offido*, if required by the bishop, to commit the unhappy victim to the flames.

"This writ," adds Blackstone,

remained still in force till the 29th of Charles the Second. And we have instances of its having been put in execution in the reigns of Elizabeth and James the First. In the 17th of Elizabeth, two Anabaptists; and in the 9th of James two Arians were thus executed.

By Statutes 9 and 10 of William the Third, if any person educated in the Christian religion, or professing the same, shall by writing, printing, teaching, or advised speaking, deny any one of the persons in the Holy Trinity to be God; or maintain that there are more Gods than one, he shall undergo the same penalties and incapacities as are inflicted upon apostacy.

"Doubtless," observes Blackstone, commenting upon the above Statutes, "the perversion of Christianity as a national religion is, abstracted from its own intrinsic truth, of the utmost consequence to the state.

I will only here just remark that, comparing the above laws with those of the Inquisition, there is nothing more cruel in the latter than in the former. But let us trace a few instances of the application of our English Code.

In the reign of Edward the Sixth, anno 1550, six Anabaptists were condemned to be burnt to death by the pious Archbishop Cranmer. One of them, Knell, was actually thus executed. The others recanted: but, as a sign that they had deserved to be burnt, they were compelled to carry *fagots*. The next year, Von Parris was equally condemned, and suffered at the stake like Knell. But the person whose fate excited chiefly the pity of the public during this reign was that of the unfortunate Joan Bocher. She was condemned to the flames—again, by Cranmer—for having maintained that Christ was not incarnate of the Virgin—not having taken any of her flesh. Edward, our historians relate, long hesitated, ere he would confirm the awful sentence. "But Cranmer," says Hume, "was employed to persuade him into compliance. And Edward, overcome by importunity, at last submitted. And the Primate, finding her obstinate, at last committed her to the flames."

It was this same Primate who was equally the chief instrument in bringing, besides Anne Askew, Joan Bocher, Von Parris, several others, both Anabaptists, Catholics, &c., to the stake. Whence, Southey himself says of him: "*Cranmer held the atrocious opinion that death by fire was the just punishment for heresy.*" Such was the founder, and chief apostle, of the Church of England. "He had been," says Neal, "a Papist, a Lutheran, and a Sacramentarian, and in every change guilty of inexcusable severities. "When he was a Lutheran, he consented to the burning of Lambert and Askew for those very doctrines for which himself afterwards suffered."—*Hist. of Puritans.*

The Second Letter

(C.)—The High Court of Commission.

Let the reader compare the tribunal of the Inquisition with the tribunal of our High Court of Commission established by Queen Elizabeth. The following is the account which Hume gives of this institution.

> Any word or writing which tended towards heresy, schism, or sedition was punishable by the High Commissioners, or any three of them. They alone were judges what expressions had that tendency. They proceeded, not by information, but by rumour, suspicion, or according to their own fancy. They administered an oath, by which the party, cited before them, was bound to answer any question which should be propounded to him. Whoever refused this oath, though under pretext that he might thereby be brought to accuse himself or his dearest friend, was punishable by imprisonment. In short, an inquisitorial tribunal, with all its terrors and iniquities, was erected in the kingdom. Full discretionary powers were bestowed with regard to inquiry, trial, sentence, and penalty inflicted.

Maclain, in his *Notes on Mosheim*, says—speaking of this said High Commission Court: "It was empowered to make inquiry, not only by legal methods, but also by rack, torture, inquisition, and imprisonment; and the fines and imprisonment to which it condemned persons were limited by no rule but its own pleasure."—Vol. iv. p. 395.

(D.)—Count Pollnitz's Testimony.

Count Pollnitz, in his entertaining *Mémoires*, addressing one of his Protestant friends, gives him the following account of the Inquisition.

> You are so deeply prejudiced against the Holy Office that I must say a few words to you upon the subject, in order—if I can do it—to disabuse you. To candid and impartial persons, this tribunal ought not to appear more formidable than any other Court of Justice. People tell a thousand tales about it—and particularly the Protestants—which

are utterly and notoriously false. Only live quietly—speak of God, and the saints, with the respect which is due to them—or at all events, do not insult them—give no public scandal—and you have then nothing at all to fear from the Holy Office. In reality, is it not the case in every country that, if men talk profanely, and act irreligiously, they would be reproved by their Consistories, if not punished by the laws? For my part, I own to you, I cannot imagine in what that barbarity consists which you Protestants attribute to the Inquisition. On the contrary, it is, in my opinion, the mildest and most lenient tribunal that exists. For, after having spoken, entertained, or committed the most injurious things against religion, provided that I but go and accuse myself of them before the Holy Office—expressing at the same time my repentance, and owning my errors—behold, the Father Commissioner—after he has represented to me the greatness of my crime, and exhorted me for the sake of my salvation to change my conduct and my opinions—at once absolves me. And where, I ask you, is the Protestant tribunal, that would be thus satisfied with the voluntary acknowledgment of a crime? Instead of thus absolving even the penitent criminal, there is, nowhere, one but what would condemn him, if not to death, at all events to prison.

I was formerly sixteen months in Rome: and during all that time, never did I so much as once hear of a single individual being arrested by the Inquisition. On the contrary, I was witness to acts of clemency in the Holy Office, such as would by no means be shown in the Consistory of Geneva. — Vol. iii.

The Third Letter

Monsieur Le Comte,

WHEN I spoke to you in my preceding letters of the origin of the Inquisition, and described its distinctive characteristics, I borrowed my account almost exclusively from the Reports of the Committee of the Cortes ordaining the suppression of this celebrated institution. I could not have given you a better proof than this of my own strict impartiality. For when, to defend a criminal, his defender derives his evidences from the very act itself of his accusation—the accuser surely, in such case, has no reason to complain.

And now, Sir, in order to make you acquainted with the nature of the proceedings of the Inquisition, I will cite to you, in the first place, the testimony of an authority which is as little to be called in question as is that of the Cortes. It is that of a learned English Protestant clergyman—the Rev. Joseph Townsend—who travelled in Spain during the years 1786–87. You may suppose that such a man, full of prejudices and animosity against everything Catholic—would not, in his descriptions, speak very favourably of the Inquisition. The following is one of his accounts, which I will request you to consider with attention. He tells us, "that at a little distance from Seville he beheld a building, the form of which struck him. Having asked a variety of questions respecting it, a person of distinction who accompanied him informed him that this strangely built edifice was called *El Quemadero*;[1] but beseeching him, at the same time, by no means to tell anyone from whom he received this information." Struck with horror at this intelligence, the humane and pious Mr. Townsend then tells us that "he at once hastened away from a spot which his imagination painted all in flames." The next

---

1 That is, the place for burning criminals.

day, he adds—a person in the office of judge communicated to him that this building was used as a scaffold for burning heretics, and that it was not more than four years ago when a female underwent this punishment. She was a nun who had been guilty of different infamous actions and crimes. Such is the narrative of this learned traveller.

Now, my Lord, only for a moment weigh some of its absurdities. In the first place, what is an edifice designed "*as a scaffold* for the burning of heretics?" Such an edifice, destined to such a purpose, would of course burn, itself, at the first experiment, and could serve but once. But an edifice, serving "*as a scaffold*" is really something so ridiculous that the imagination can fancy nothing more preposterous. And then, how exceedingly amusing is the grave recommendation of the distinguished personage, requesting the Rev. traveller "not to reveal the secret!"—a secret concerning a public building, designed for the execution of criminals *by fire*! Such as these are the pitiful tales by which ignorance and bigotry impose upon the credulity and weakness of the public. I have no doubt but the gravity of the Spaniard, upon this occasion, must have pitied, or rather ridiculed, the absurdity of the man whose protestant piety could have swallowed so much nonsense. "*You see,*" some good-natured wit of Seville would have said to him—"*you see this building, Sir; it is here that they burn heretics, in great secrecy. But pray, for the love of God, don't say anything about it; else, you would ruin me.*" (A)

It is, again, not a little entertaining to remark that our traveller speaks of the *Quemadero*, just as if it were a coffee roaster, every day in use. His imagination (it is really so) represents this building to him, "as a place surrounded with flames of blood." You would suppose it a slaughter-house in the middle of a permanent and constantly burning funeral pile. And yet, for four years, it had never once witnessed an execution! And then, too, what was the victim? "It was a nun, convicted of different infamous crimes and profanations."

And where then, tell me, is the nation where justice does not visit such crimes as hers? The pious traveller has not thought proper to enter into any details. But his expressions leave open a wide, strange, latitude: and it is really entertaining to hear him, first, confidently assert that the place is destined for the burning of heretics; and then, immediately after, cite as a proof of this, not the execution of a heretic, but of a monster.

In certain wise and well-regulated states of Europe, the law

The Third Letter

is that the incendiary of an inhabited house, shall, himself, be condemned to the flames; and the public in general say: "*He very well deserves it.*" But, at all events, think you, Sir, that the person who is guilty of a variety of infamous crimes, both in practice and in theory, is less criminal, in fact, than an incendiary?

But I will cite to you another example of Mr. Townsend's abhorrence, and reprobation, of the Inquisition. It is the account of a very frightful Auto-da-fé which took place a little while before his Reverence arrived in Spain.

"A beggar," he tells us,

> named Ignazio Rodriguez, was condemned by the tribunal of the Inquisition for having distributed certain love potions of a very indecent nature; and of having, in the administration of the infamous remedy, pronounced certain words of necromancy. It was, moreover, proved that he had administered the disgusting dose to all ranks of persons. Rodriguez had two accomplices in his crimes, who were equally condemned as he was—their names, Juliana Lopez, and Angela Barrios. One of these imploring the judges to spare her life—they told her, '*that it was not the practice of the Holy Office to condemn anyone to death.*' Rodriguez was condemned to be led through the streets of Madrid, mounted on an ass, and to be whipped. They likewise imposed upon him certain practices of religion; and to be banished from the Capital for five years. The reading of the sentence was frequently interrupted by peals of laughter, in which the beggar himself joined.

"Accordingly, the criminal was led through the streets, but not whipped. On the way, and during the procession, the people offered him wine and biscuits," (cruel creatures) "to refresh him." Such is the narrative given by Mr. Townsend.

Now, I do think that nothing can well be more lenient and humane than all this process. If here the tribunal deserves any reproach, it is for the excess of its indulgence. For, if we only consider the words of the traveller, we find that the *ingredients* employed by Rodriguez were such as would, in any other country, have condemned him to the pillory, to the galleys, or even to the gallows.

However, all this does not satisfy Mr. Townsend. "The crime," he remarks, "was far below the dignity of the tribunal, and that it would have been much better to have punished the miserable wretch *in secret*, by the vilest minister of justice."

It may, no doubt, be the case that this said Mr. Townsend *may have been, once*—or *may be* so still—a very sensible man. But where national prejudices and religious bigotry prevail, there good sense is completely useless. Strange it is to see a man insolently reprobating the criminal jurisprudence of a distinguished nation, and at the same time himself recommending the adoption of *secret punishments*. Had the Inquisition ordered one single lash of the whip to be inflicted *secretly*, our traveller, in this case, would have loudly inveighed against such atrocity, and have enriched his work with a beautiful engraving, in which he would have exhibited two huge, robust, executioners, tearing, with furious strokes, the flesh of the unhappy victim, in the depth of some frightful dungeon, and in the presence of some pious Dominicans.

Is it not, my Lord—I ask you—a piece of insolent presumption in a traveller—a mere stranger—to undertake to decide, without any knowledge of the cause, what a great tribunal of Spain should either publish or conceal, according to the nature of the crimes which are brought before it, and the degree of publicity which human wickedness has stamped upon them? Surely the tribunals of Spain, like those of other nations, are the best judges of what it is proper either to conceal or to expose to the public.

The rest of the reproaches of the Reverend traveller concerning the Inquisition are not less groundless than the preceding. He says, for example, "that this tribunal can cite before it whomsoever it thinks proper; nay, that it can even surprise and seize people in their beds in the middle of the night."

If here it be Mr. Townsend's intention to speak of *witnesses*, he, in this case, betrays the grossest ignorance of criminal justice. For, if anything can do honour to any government—anything that can prove its strength and impartiality—it is the authority which it gives to its tribunals to cite before them such witnesses as they think necessary to determine the justice of any cause. It is so in England—as, in fact, it is so in every civilized nation. Men, if summoned, are everywhere obliged to appear before their respective courts of justice; to give testimony; and to submit, sometimes, to very painful,

The Third Letter

and tedious interrogatories. But so it is—when there is question of Spain, principles are altered. *Justice here is injustice; and right is wrong.*

But if it be the design of Mr. Townsend to speak of the accused—here he is more ridiculous still. For, let the person, be who he may—why, if he be accused of any crime—why ought he not to be cited or arrested accordingly as circumstances require? Strange, indeed, would be the privilege that exempted anyone, or such and such individuals, from the jurisdiction or action of the tribunals. But the circumstance which, beyond any other, hurts the feelings of our traveller, is this—"*that the person accused may be arrested in the night, and even in his bed!*" This, above all the atrocities of the Inquisition, is what most excites his indignation. In England, it may be the case that a debtor, for example, or a person guilty only of some small offence, may not, or cannot, be arrested in the middle of the night and in bed. But I do not believe that such can be the case whenever there is question of a capital crime. Or if such be the case, I can only say—"so much the worse for England." And I do not see, why Spain is so far obliged to respect the sleep of a set of villains.

We have just seen the preparations for the frightful Auto-da-fé, which took place in 1764, in virtue of which an infamous criminal was condemned to eat biscuits and drink wine through the streets of Madrid. But let us now, still farther, see how our good Protestant relates the terms in which the Grand Inquisitor addressed the impious wretch, and announced to him the sentence of the Holy Office. Mr. Townsend's account of it is not a little amusing.

"My Son," said the Inquisitor, with the greatest mildness, "you are going to hear the relation of your crimes, and the sentence pronounced for the expiation of your guilt. Our lenity is great, because our holy tribunal, always most indulgent, seeks rather to reform than to punish. Let your sorrow flow from the consciousness of guilt, and not from a sense of the disgrace you suffer."

The monster was accordingly, as I have stated, marched through the streets of Madrid, eating biscuits and drinking wine. And the pious traveller adds—Oh horrible cruelty!—that "the first nobility, and all the ladies of the court, were invited to be present at the ceremony by the Marquise de Cogulludo—who also, after it, gave a grand entertainment to the judges and officers of the Inquisition."

He closes his interesting narrative with the following reflection, which, if anything of this kind could do so—ought somewhat to surprise us in this travelling Minister of the Gospel.

"If the King," he says, "wishing to destroy the tribunal, intended to render it contemptible in the eyes of his subjects, he could not have adopted a better expedient."

Thus, then, the admirable alliance of legal severity with Christian charity—the compassion of the public, corresponding with the clemency of the judges—the paternal address and discourse of the Inquisitor; the sentence of condemnation no other than an exhortation to the criminal to reform his life—the punishment which followed changed all at once into a feast of mercy, which the nobility came to celebrate, in company with the judges—all this mild and tender jurisprudence—and which is so remarkable, and so peculiar to Spain—neither awakes the admiration, nor yet the slenderest interest, of a man whose eye is clouded, and whose reason is vitiated, by the unhappy prejudices of his nation. On the contrary, in the whole process, and in a spectacle that would have excited the admiration of a Muhammadan, or a Hindu—had they properly understood it—our enlightened traveller sees nothing but objects of ridicule and motives for contempt.

I hope, my Lord, that I have now said sufficient to give you a correct idea of the origin, the nature, the true character and proceedings of the Inquisition. There is, however, another circumstance which well deserves your serious attention. It is this—that the tribunal of the Inquisition, which is thus so grossly calumniated and reviled, was in fact rendered a real *Court of Equity*, at least equally necessary in the *criminal* order of things as it was in the *civil*.

Grotius has defined *equity*—"*Correctio ejus, in quo lex, propter universalitatem, deficit*,"—that is, "the remedy invented for those cases in which the law, on account of its universality, is deficient." This definition is the dictate only of a great mind. Man can make only general laws. And for this very reason, they are, of their own nature, in part, unjust; because they cannot reach and apply to every possible case. Whence it is true, that *the exception to the rule* is, under these circumstances, alike and equally *just*, as is the rule itself. And wherever there is neither dispensation, exception, nor mitigation, there must necessarily, in such cases, exist violation and abuses: because

The Third Letter

universal conscience allowing, at first, the establishment of exceptions—soon, individual passions interfere to generalise them, in order to defeat the law.

In the criminal order of things, the power of equity is usually confided, and confined, to the Sovereign. Hence, the grant of pardons; the commutation of punishments; Lettres de Cachet, &c., in room of legal condemnations; economical judgments, &c. But it is a point which every enlightened observer knows, and will admit, that the interference of the Sovereign's power in the administration of justice, is, of all things, the most dangerous. Not that I wish—God forbid that I should—to call in question the Sovereign's claim to the happy and magnificent right of granting pardon. What alone I contend for is that he ought to make use of the prerogative with prudence and great sobriety, lest, by exerting it too far, he create greater evils. I think that whenever there is not any question of pardon, properly so called, but of certain mitigations, which it is not easy to define—but above all with respect to such crimes as violate religion and public morals—I think that, in these cases, the mitigating power would, with far greater advantage, be vested in an enlightened tribunal, at once essentially *royal*; and at the same time, in the quality of its judges, *sacerdotal*. For, what can possibly be imagined more reasonable and proper than to introduce "*the Oil of Mercy*" amid the angry and violent discussions of criminal jurisprudence?

Considered in this point of view, the Inquisition, it is certain, is so formed as to render great service to the public. For example, it may be remembered that, not many years ago, a very infamous female in Madrid, had—by the appearance of the most heroic piety, but concealing the deepest and the most refined hypocrisy—contrived to deceive the whole capital. She had for her pretended director, and her real accomplice, a monk, still more wicked and abandoned than herself. Such was the excess of her criminal artifices, that she imposed upon the credulity of a certain bishop; and pretending that she was too ill to leave her chamber, obtained leave, through his interest and application, to have the Blessed Sacrament preserved in it, for the alleged exercise of her devotions. It was, however, ere long, discovered that this said apartment was the scene and theatre of the most criminal disorders. Here, then, the Inquisition, informed of the crimes, and taking to itself the cognisance of them, had the fairest opportunity of displaying a magnificent Auto-da-fé against the two criminals, and above all against the monk. However, even on this awful occasion, justice could not entirely supersede mercy. The Inquisition disposed of the abandoned woman without any éclat, punished her accomplice without putting him to death, and screened the reputation of the unsuspecting prelate whose credulity had been so shamefully imposed upon.

I will cite to you another example. The history of two ecclesiastics—the brothers Questas—was very well known throughout Spain. They had the misfortune to have displeased a celebrated favourite at Court; and were, through his interest, made over to the Inquisition, charged with an accusation which was supported by all the weight of an influence which seemed to be invincible. In short, nothing was forgotten or omitted, that ingenuity could imagine or invent, to ruin the two individuals. But the Inquisitor of Valladolid, by some means or other, got wind of the conspiracy; and neither any ascendency of authority, nor any seductions of persuasion, could move him from his determination to follow up the cause of justice. He suspected, and sifted carefully, the accusations alleged against the two brothers, and having procured fresh testimony, he declared both of them innocent. The business was then carried by appeal before the supreme tribunal of the Inquisition at Madrid. And here, too, the Grand Inquisitor resisted nobly the giant child of favour and obtained the victory over him. One of the brothers, who had been imprisoned, was set at liberty, and the other, who had taken flight, returned quietly to his friends.

On another occasion, previous to the aforesaid instance, the Grand Inquisitor, Aveda, making the visit of the prisons of the Inquisition, found in them certain individuals hitherto unknown to him. "*And who,*" he said, "*are these men?*" — "*They are men,*" was the reply, "*who have been arrested by the orders of government, and sent into these prisons for such and such a cause.*" — "*Well,*" remarked the Inquisitor, "*but all this* has nothing to do with religion." And he accordingly ordered them to be released.

Besides the aforesaid accounts, which I have learnt from the most unquestionable authority, it would be easy to adduce a thousand others which, like them, attest the happy influence of the Inquisition, considered at once as a Court of Equity, as an instrument of national policy, and as an organ

The Third Letter

of censure. It is, in fact, in this threefold point of view that this Institution ought properly to be considered. For, at times, its gentler influences serve to mitigate the severity and the often ill-graduated inflictions of the criminal law. In some instances, it enables the Sovereignty to exercise, with less inconvenience than it can do in any other tribunal, a certain kind of justice which, under one form or other, exists in every country. In short, on many occasions—more fortunate and successful than the tribunals of other nations—the tribunal of the Inquisition represses vice and immorality in a way, of all others, the most useful to the state—threatening, whenever any disorder becomes notorious, or alarming—to efface the line which separates *the sin* from *the crime*.

It is my firm conviction that a tribunal of the above description, modified according to times, places, and the character of nations, would be, everywhere—in every kingdom—peculiarly useful. At all events, it has certainly rendered to Spain the most signal services, and this illustrious kingdom owes to it the tribute of immortal thanks. This, however, is a point which I propose to establish in my succeeding letter, so as to leave, I flatter myself, no doubt upon your Lordship's mind.

Notes and Illustrations.

(A.) English Travellers.

THERE is no set of men under the sun who correspond so exactly with the character of Rabelais' Lamian Witches as do our English travellers. "These witches," says Rabelais, "are so sharp-sighted and lynx-eyed, when they are *from home*, that they can see everything—can see objects which had never before been observed, nor so much as heard of. Whereas, when they are *at home*, they can see nothing—they are downright blind. The case is that, *when at home, they regularly and always put their eyes into their shoes.*"

Such precisely as this is the character, and such the case, particularly of our *English* travellers: for, the travellers of other nations are neither, when *from home*, so keen sighted, nor when at home, so blind, as ours are. Our travellers—true Lamians—in their journeys, and tours, and voyages to different countries, discover an endless, countless multitude of the strangest and most astonishing things that were ever heard of—monsters, chimeras, &c.—which no human being but themselves had ever so much as suspected to exist. Hence, therefore, their very interesting volumes are full of the most important discoveries—beings, and scenes, and actions, and objects alike curious and wonderful as they are important. These important discoveries relate principally, however, to the Catholic religion—to the professors, the follies, the vices, the superstitions, the bigotry, &c., of what they call "Popery." And then, it is equally true that the descriptions which they give of these things are so eloquent—their tales of wonder are so admirably told—as to excite the delight of the pious Protestant, and to confirm him in the orthodoxy of his faith—whilst, indeed, some of their tales are so frightful as to terrify the pious ladies, and half the old women of the nation. A Book of Travels, without these recommendations—and our Lamians know it well, would be lifeless, and insipid—it would hardly find a reader. Hence, therefore—for, the trade is, moreover, a very profitable one—hence, the quick-sightedness of these men in seeing, and their zeal and eloquence in describing what they represent as the Catholic religion. The real fact, however, is—that their representations and accounts are, for the far greater part, neither more nor less than a tissue of silly lies and pitiful tales—the dictates of prejudice, and the inventions of bigotry and interest. "There is no wonder," says Dr. Moore,

> that the English are peculiarly prejudiced in their notions of foreign countries, and still more so in regard to the religious tenets of foreign nations. Well stocked with prejudices, before they begin to travel, they are always sure to look out for those objects which confirm them [...] Many English travellers remain four or five years abroad; and during all that space, have hardly been ever in any other company but that of their own countrymen. — *Travels through France.*

It would be easy, indeed, to adduce the testimony of a *few* of our travellers—for, they are not, every one of them, Lamian Witches—reprobating the conduct and the prejudices of their fellow-travelling countrymen. Thus, the candid Mr. Temple says:

> Every Englishman must own, after a little travelling, and mixing in foreign society, that our own prejudices, whether as a nation or a sect, appear to us as unworthy and inveterate as those of any under the sun. They will admit that no set of men, in their private character, have been so injuriously aspersed by the cankered tongue of slander, as the Roman Catholic priesthood, &c. — *Travels.*

If the tales of our travellers were read only by the candid and enlightened, so far from wishing to check, I should wish rather to promote their circulation—because, to such minds, the reading of them would suggest only the feelings of contempt and of reprobation for so much injustice. In like manner, if their accounts and tales did us no injury, we should, in this case, laugh at them as so many subjects of amusement. But, unhappily, so it is—the number of enlightened Protestants, in regard of our religion, approaches, I fear, very near to zero—"*Malunt nescire, quia jam oderunt.*" ["They do not know what they have a mind to hate."] Whereas, the multitudes who read the lies and fictions of our travellers are immense— in fact, nearly all who can read at all. These, therefore, receive and read them with greediness. They look upon their falsehoods as so many truths—their ridicule, as so much wit—and their insults, as so much orthodoxy. Thus it is that the public form their notions of our religion, and thus contract their prejudices and their hostility against it. Calumny, indeed, insult and ridicule, are awful things. They prove everything to the ignorant, the prejudiced, and the weak.

If I were disposed to do so, how easy would it be for me to draw a picture of this Protestant country, which, for the darkness of its shades, and the horror of its scenes, would at least equal those descriptions which our travellers give of Catholic nations. Our daily papers, indeed, as well as a multitude of Protestant writers—for, *all* are not Lamians—present to us constantly such proofs of vice; of ignorance; of irreligion, of fanaticism, &c., as would, I think, be looked for in vain in any other Christian country.

Thus, for example, in regard of *vice*—take only, as a specimen, the account which, in his *Letter to the Bishop of London*, the Rev. Mr. Noel gives of the state of our capital. This boasted seat of wisdom contains, he asserts—"its 500,000 Sabbath breakers, at the very least, its 10,000 enslaved gamblers, its 20,000 beggars; its 30,000 thieves, its 100,000 habitual drunkards; its 100,000 systematic and abandoned profligates." The proportion of these disorders will, of course, be somewhat less in the provinces than in a capital. Still, the fact will not be denied that they are, everywhere—but above all in our manufacturing towns—in a very frightful degree prevalent. And then, too, what is equally the case—vice in this country is far bolder and more unblushing than it is in other nations; for, in these, however prevalent it may be, it is, at all events, far more retired, and more modest.

In regard of the *Neglect of Religion*. Bishop Porteus, in one of his Charges says: "Scarcely one symptom of religion ever appears amongst us, except on the Lord's Day." Addison—when the sense of religion was more common than it is at present—observes, in his *Freeholder*: "There is less religion in England than in any other country—a fact," he adds, "which all travellers must have remarked, who take any notice of what passes in other nations." — "We are acquainted with no country in Europe," says the learned writer of the *Black Book*, "in which abuses are more prevalent, and in which there is so little piety."

In regard of *Ignorance*. Bishop Porteus again, lamenting the

The Third Letter

dreadful evil—states that, "In some parts of his diocese, the people are in a state little short of Pagan ignorance and irreligion." He tells us that, in his own living, which he held in the country, "he found his parishioners absolutely ignorant of the God who made them."—In like manner, the pious Hannah More—in her *Letters*—complains as follows: "While we are sending missionaries to India, our own villages are in Pagan darkness, and upon many of them scarcely a ray of Christianity has shone." — "The populace of England," say the writers of the *Quarterly Review*, "are more ignorant of their religious duties than they are in any other Christian country."

In regard of *Infidelity*. "Infidelity, and Indifference," say the writers of the *British Critic*—there is no better authority—"are the prevailing and damning sins of the nation." Voltaire, indeed, was so convinced of the prevalence of these misfortunes in this country, that in one of his *Letters to D'Alembert*, he exultingly exclaims—"*Nous avons pour nous Toute L'Angleterre.*" ["We have for ourselves the whole of England."]

In regard of *Sects, and the Confusion of Religions*—certain it is that in no nation of the universe do there prevail half so many as there do in this country; whence, also, it is proverbially called by the French—"*Le pays des Sectes.*" ["The Land of Sects"] And then, too, these sects prevail in every shape and shade of error, from the absurdities of fanaticism to the impieties of irreligion. Edwards, in his *Gangræna*, cited by Dr. Gray, once reckoned up "a hundred and seventy-six heretical and blasphemous opinions maintained in this country *in the course of four years.*" In fact, so numberless and various are the sects and religions of this country—forming an immense circle of absurdity and error—that I defy any learning to count them up. Just like the Shades of Virgil, they have pressed, and still press upon each other, at the gates of Oblivion—"*Huc omnis turba effusa ruebat*"—*et ruit*. ["Here rushed all the throng pouring out—and rushes."]

As a proof altogether of the *Fanaticism, Superstition, Ignorance, Credulity, &c.*, which prevail in this country, I might cite the fact which but yesterday came—not, perhaps, to excite the wonder of those who know the general state of its society—but, to give pain to the pious and well instructed. A madman, calling himself Sir William Courtenay, announced himself the saviour of the world; the Messiah, invested with a divine mission—Jesus Christ himself, who had been crucified upon the cross. And in order to make this latter pretext the more credible, he made certain punctures, or appearances of punctures, in his hands and side, as the wounds inflicted on the occasion of his Passion. He, moreover, besides all this, represented himself as invulnerable—or that, if he were shot, he should shortly revive again.

Now, profane and absurd as all this was—yet it was all firmly and piously believed. The man's blasphemies were revered as so many heavenly truths—his pretended invulnerability as an undoubted miracle, and his promised resuscitation as a positive fact. Neither did this infatuation cease, even when the wretched fanatic was killed. For, (I quote the account, as given in the *St. James's Chronicle*, at the time) "his blouse, or smock-frock, stained with blood, was torn up with pious ardour *by the thousands of his admirers* who crowded to see his body. His hair and beard also were eagerly seized, and placed in the hands of the Canterbury jewellers to fashion them into brooches, &c. Two oak trees, which stand adjacent to the spot in which he fell, were stripped of their bark for relics. Even the blood-stained earth, in the several spots, where he and his followers fell, has been scraped up and carried off as sacred mementoes."

If the profaneness and folly of all this had been confined to a few ignorant and deluded fanatics, the thing might not excite much wonder. But we here see, as the journalist states, that they pervaded and infected *thousands*—and, of course, a considerable number of individuals whose circumstances and situation in life were respectable and decent. This, indeed, is admitted.

Such, then, even in this *enlightened* nation, as it is called—such, in a county which Shakespeare once called "the civilest in our isle"—such, under the very shade of Canterbury's hallowed towers, and within the atmosphere of two illustrious bishoprics, where piety—if anywhere—ought to reign, and instruction flourish—such, even under all these favourable circumstances, is the state of the public mind—at all events, among the vulgar—on the subject of religion. In no nation, I am convinced, would our travellers meet anywhere with instances of ignorance, fanaticism, and folly, parallel or similar to the above.

But, in fact, to show the ignorance and fanaticism of the English people, I might have appealed to instances—and these, too, very recent ones—perhaps even more astonishing than the above. Such, for example, was the case of Johanna

The Third Letter

Southcote, whose miraculous conception, heavenly parturition, and divine resuscitation, were piously believed, not only by thousands of the vulgar, but even by many of the best instructed—nay, even by certain clergymen of the Established Church. Such, again, but yesterday, was the case of the raving Irving, and his Angels. The howlings of the former, and the unknown tongues of the latter, were listened to and revered as the voice of God, and the dictates of the will of heaven—and this, again, by multitudes of the well instructed. Even the Mountebank ravings, which are now so constantly taking place in Exeter Hall, are specimens of fanaticism, ignorance, bigotry, and superstition such as nowhere can now be found but in this enlightened nation.

Wherefore, having thus stated a few of the many disorders which prevail in this country, I will simply here remark that if our travellers did not, like the Lamian Witches, put their eyes into their shoes, they might find as much to condemn and ridicule "*at home*," as they do when "*from home*," to reprobate and vilify.

The Fourth Letter

Monsieur Le Comte,

IN the natural sciences, there is always question of *mean quantities*. Thus, we speak of the *mean* distance, the *mean* movement, the *mean* duration, &c. It would be well if this same notion were applied also to politics, and that men would feel, and be convinced, that the best institutions are not those which present the greatest degree of possible happiness at such or such a given period, *but those which ensure the greatest sum or measure of possible happiness to the greatest number of possible generations! This*—and I think the point quite evident—is *mean* happiness.

Upon this principle, I should be curious, and should like to know what the bitterest enemy of the Inquisition would reply to the Spaniard, who, passing over what I have just said—should undertake to defend it, in terms like the following.

> "Sir," he says to the supposed accuser, "you are *Myops*—you are short-sighted, and see but a single object. Our legislators looked down from an eminence and saw the great whole. At the opening of the sixteenth century they beheld Europe, as it were, in flames. In order to secure themselves from the general conflagration, they employed the Inquisition—which is the *political instrument* they made use of, both to preserve the unity of faith, and to prevent the wars of religion. You have done nothing like this. But now trace and remark the result. I appeal but to experience: for, experience is the best criterion to direct men's judgment.
>
> "Behold, then, the thirty years' war, enkindled by the doctrines of Luther. Look at the unheard-of excesses of the Anabaptists—the civil wars of France, of England, and of Holland. Consider the massacres

of the St. Bartholomew; of Merindal; and the Cevennes—the murder of Queen Mary Stuart—that of Henry the Third; of Henry the Fourth; of Charles the First; of the Prince of Orange, &c. A ship might float in the ocean of blood which your innovators have shed. The Inquisition would have punished only these disturbers of the public peace and order. It ill becomes you, ignorant and presumptuous as you are—you who had foreseen nothing, and have deluged Europe in blood—it ill becomes you to blame our monarchs, who had foreseen everything, and secured their kingdom from devastation. Don't tell me that the Inquisition has produced such and such abuses, at such and such a time. This is not the question. The question is, to know whether, during the last three centuries, there has been, by virtue of the Inquisition, a greater enjoyment of peace and happiness in Spain, than in the other nations of Europe? To sacrifice present generations to the problematic happiness of future generations—this may be the calculation of a philosopher, but it is not that of an enlightened legislator.

"But, if this observation do not suffice to convince you, I will, then, appeal to what we have witnessed during the late conflicts with the gigantic power of France, wielded by the greatest of all modern conquerors and heroes. It was the Inquisition which then—far beyond any other instrument, saved Spain, and immortalised it. It preserved, and kept alive, that public spirit, that faith, that religious patriotism which produced those wonders which we have all witnessed; and which, it may be, by saving Spain, saved Europe itself from tyranny and oppression. From the summits of the Pyrennees, the Inquisition frightened away that profane philosophism which had, it is true, its good reasons for hating the Institution. Its eye was always open, watching the dangerous works, which, like so many dreadful avalanches, fell down from the mountains. And although, unhappily, too many of these poisonous instruments did escape its vigilance, and serve to seduce and corrupt a considerable number of individuals—still, the great body of the people

> remained faithful and unimpaired. It was the Inquisition alone that could restore—and that actually, far beyond any other aid, did restore, (such was the noble ardour which it inspired)—the monarch to his throne."

For my part, I do not see what reasonable reply could well be made to these striking observations. What here, however, is extraordinary, and I believe, very little known—is the complete apology for the Inquisition, made by Voltaire himself; and which I will lay before you as a remarkable monument of that *good sense*, which sees and admits *facts*; and at the same time, of that prejudice, which is blind to their *causes*.

"During the sixteenth and the seventeenth centuries," says Voltaire,

> there were not, in Spain, any of those sanguinary revolutions; of those conspiracies; of those cruelties, which were so common in the other nations of Europe. Neither the Duke of Lerma nor the Count Olivares ever shed the blood of their enemies upon the scaffold. Kings were never assassinated there; neither did any of them perish there, as they did in England, by the hand of the executioner. *In short, were it not for the horrors of the Inquisition, there was nothing then wherewith Spain could be reproached.*

No blindness, surely, can be well greater than this. Without the "horrors" of the Inquisition, there would be no room to cast any reproach upon Spain—which, *only by the power and influences of the Inquisition, escaped those horrors which disgraced every other nation!* Thus—and I rejoice at the circumstance—thus does genius chastise itself—condemned to descend to the lowest absurdity, even to the most pitiful nonsense—as a just punishment for having prostituted itself to the defence of error. I am less gratified with the natural superiority of men's talents than with their nullity, whenever they forget their proper destination.

After witnessing all the horrors which have disgraced and afflicted Europe—how, or with what face, can men reproach Spain for having possessed an institution which would effectually have prevented them all? *The Holy Office, with but sixty sentences or trials in a century, would have saved us the frightful spectacle of those heaps of human bodies—mountain-high as the Alps; and sufficient to stop the course of the Rhine and the Po.* But, of all Europeans, the French—considering the calamities which they have brought upon the world; and the still more dreadful evils which they brought upon themselves—the French are, beyond all dispute, the most unpardonable critics of the Inquisition—ridiculing Spain, as some of their writers do, for the very wisdom of the institutions which alone had so long preserved it. Let us do justice to this illustrious nation—she is one of the few nations that never became an accomplice of the French revolution. She did, indeed, at length, become its victim. But the blood of four hundred thousand strangers sufficiently avenged her cause, and the Spaniard again resumed his ancient maxims.

The Committee of the Cortes, whom I have cited already, were fully sensible of the force of the argument in favour of the Inquisition, which results from the consideration of the evidence that its tribunal prevented the introduction of innumerable evils into the country. In order, however, to elude this powerful attestation, the reporter of the said Committee has ingeniously found out an expeditious and convenient expedient—which is at once to deny the influence of the Inquisition. "*The authority of the bishops,*" he says, "*had this only been preserved—would have sufficed to defend Spain against the late heresiarchs. It is not to the Inquisition that we are indebted for this happiness.*" — (Report, p. 77)

Now, Sir, only remark how little prejudice and passion, pay attention to what they say. You have seen already, in my preceding letter (the second) that the bishops, so far from complaining of the Inquisitors, considered them, on the contrary, "as their faithful allies," in the preservation of the purity of faith. But conceding everything to the Committee—that it may itself refute itself—if the ordinary authority of the bishops was, alone, sufficient to repel error, and to secure Spain from the intrusions of heresy—how comes it that this same authority, usurped by the Inquisition, and moreover, increased and improved by a multitude of important reforms—how comes it—or how imagine—that this said institution has been of no use to Spain? The fact is certain, and notorious, that our modern heresiarchs could never set foot in Spain. Surely, then, something must have sufficed to prevent their intrusion. Now, what was this something, that *sufficed* for this useful purpose? It was not the power of the bishops, since the Inquisition had deprived them of it. Neither, according to the Committee of the Cortes, was it the Inquisition itself. Again, it was not to the civil tribunals, nor to the governors of the provinces, &c., that the above benefits are to be attributed: because the Inquisition possessed the exclusive jurisdiction in all matters relating to religion. Therefore, once more—since something or other did *suffice*—what was this all-sufficient instrument? If the Committee did not see this, the sole reason must have been that they shut their eyes and would not see it. But I defy any man who has eyes and is willing to see, not to be convinced that, since every European nation—Spain alone, and certain states which had more or less adopted the jurisdiction and forms of the Inquisition, excepted—it is consequently but just and reasonable to attribute the preservation and peace of Spain to the power and influence—and to the power and influence alone—of the Inquisition—above all, since no other cause can be assigned. Suppose, for example, that, in the fourteenth century, one single nation had, alone, escaped that dreadful pestilence which then desolated Europe. If this fortunate country hereafter boasted that it possessed a system of prophylactics—a remedy, announced and prepared for the salutary effect—a remedy, long and constantly made use of, and whose healthy and preservative ingredients it was willing to make known—it surely would in such case be utterly unreasonable to tell such nation that it owed nothing to the boasted remedy, and that other remedies would have equally sufficed for the same purpose—whereas all other remedies neither had, nor would have anywhere sufficed, save in this one nation alone.

In making this apology for the Inquisition, I should pass over an important circumstance if I did not request you to remark the influence of this institution upon the Spanish character. If this nation so long preserved its maxims, its unity of faith, its public spirit, it was solely to the Inquisition that it owed these benefits. For, only look at that miserable host of men who had been formed in the schools of modern philosophy. What did these men do for Spain? *Evil*, and nothing else but *evil*. They alone called in, or promoted, tyranny. They alone, instead of rousing a noble resistance, and a spirit of unshaken fidelity—preached only those half measures which had well nigh ruined the nation—obedience to the empire of circumstances; timidity; weakness, delays, concessions, &c. If Spain be ever destined to perish, it is these, or such men as these, that will prove the authors of her ruin. There are, indeed, multitudes of superficial men who believe, and have contended, that in her late struggles, she was saved by the Cortes: whereas, she was saved directly *in spite* of the Cortes. It was *the people* that did everything. There were, it may be, among the enemies of the Inquisition, and among the partisans of philosophy, a few individuals—true Spaniards—who were capable of laying down their lives for their country. But what could these men have done without the *people?* And, in their turn, what could, or would, the people have done, had they not been led on by their national ideas; and animated, above all, by what men now call "*Superstition?*" If you wish to extinguish that enthusiasm which inspires great thoughts, and impels to noble enterprises—if you wish to render men's hearts cold and unfeeling, and to substitute egotism in the room of generous and ardent patriotism—if you wish to do this, only take away from the people their *faith*, and make them philosophers.

There is not, in Europe, one single nation, or one body of people, so little known, or so much calumniated, as the Spaniards. *Spanish superstition* is become a proverb. And yet nothing is more groundless. The higher orders of the nation are as well educated and as enlightened as we are. In regard of the lower classes, it may be, for example, in relation to the veneration paid to the saints, or rather to their images—it may be that they sometimes, and here and there, exceed the measure of wise devotion. But, as here the dogma itself is neither violated, nor denied—so the trifling abuses, prevailing amongst a certain portion of the ignorant and the simple, matter very little in these regards—nay, they are not even—as I could easily show you, without their advantages. But, at all events, this is true—that the Spaniard has less prejudice and fewer superstitions than those very people who laugh at him without ever having reflected upon themselves. Thus, you know, I dare say, a number of respectable individuals in the first ranks of society, who sincerely and firmly believe in amulets, apparitions, sympathetic remedies, dreams, fortune-tellers, and many such like fooleries. You have seen persons refuse to sit at table where, unfortunately, the number of the invited guests was twelve—who would change colour if an unlucky waiter chanced profanely to overturn the salt-cellar—who, upon no consideration whatsoever, would set out on a journey on such or such a day, &c. Well, Sir, go into Spain. There you will be surprised to meet with none of these silly and humiliating superstitions. The reason is that as real religious principle is essentially opposed to all such empty fancies and beliefs—so, wheresoever it prevails, it is sure always to despise and disregard them. At the same time, it is also true that the contempt of such follies is founded more or less upon the national good sense of the Spaniard.

But, after all, there is no mercy for Spain. Not only do the English writers in particular incessantly inveigh against the Inquisition; but even its ministers declared in Parliament (this was in the year 1814), that "they had done everything in their power, by way of remonstrances and representations, to oppose the *shameful* measures of the Spanish authorities, and above all, the re-establishment of the *detestable Inquisition.*"

Now, for my own part—and I say it with all the sincerity of my feelings, and after reflecting upon what I have written upon the subject—for my own part, I cannot discover what there is so "*detestable*" in this famous Institution. However, an accusation so solemn as the above, and made in so honourable an assembly, calls upon me to devote to it a few particular observations. I hope, therefore, in the succeeding letter, to convince your Lordship that, amid all the nations of Europe, the English have the least right to reproach Spain with its Inquisition. You will read and judge. (A).

Notes and Illustrations.

(A.) Persecution is not a Catholic Tenet.

IT has been sufficiently demonstrated, in the series of the preceding letters, that the Inquisition is a political institution, and that although it did, sometimes, inflict the penalty of death upon heretics—yet it was not the spiritual members of this tribunal who passed this sentence, or who even so much as concurred in it. They had, indeed—as the nature of their office compelled them to do—examined, in the case of the accused, the allegations which were brought against him, and where the evidences of his heretical or infidel opinions were manifest and incontestable, they but simply declared them such. With the subsequent punishments inflicted upon the criminal, they had nothing at all to do. These were the business of the civil power alone.

However, as the Tribunal was composed of a certain number of ecclesiastical and religious members, it has, for this reason, pleased the injustice and the prejudices of our English writers not only to impute to these all the odium of its alleged cruelties, but even to contend that the persecution of heretics is one of the tenets of our religion. This accusation may be found in almost every work that has been composed against our religion. It has been, of late—and it is so still, with mischievous effect, bawled into the ears of the public, in different halls, taverns, &c., by a set of holy, and for the most part, well paid, fanatics. Nay, it is even re-echoed constantly through those walls where nothing but the language of charity and the voice of justice should be heard.

Now, the real fact is that persecution, so far from being a tenet of the Catholic Church, is a direct violation, both of its maxims and its professions. For, so far from *claiming* any right to punish heretics with death, she positively *disclaims* any such prerogative or power. The principle which she adopts and maintains is that of Tertullian: "*It belongs not to religion, to force religion.*" According to the dictates of its Canon law, so averse is the Church to the spilling of human blood that no one can be promoted to any Holy Orders, nor exercise the duties of Holy Orders, who has even concurred to the death or mutilation of any human being—although such acts had taken place, either on the occasion of a just war, or under the circumstances of a judicial proceeding. Thus, whenever any ecclesiastical judge or spiritual tribunal pronounced, or pronounces, any individual guilty of obstinate heresy, or impiety, such judge or tribunal declared, or declares, at the same time, that their authority extends no farther than such decision. It was so even in the case of John Huss. The Council of Constance, after having convicted him of heresy, declared that beyond this, its power was void, and of no effect.

We may trace the spirit of the Church during those periods—the Middle Ages, for example—when its authority was raised to the highest pitch. During those ages, although it condemned heresies and schisms, and excommunicated the authors and promoters of them, yet, it never inflicted upon these men either the penalty of death, nor yet any corporal punishment at all. It was so in the cases of Felix D'Urgel, Goteschalk, Berengarius, Abelard, Marsilius of Padua, Wycliff, &c. The Church never visited these heresiarchs by any bodily inflictions.

It is remarked by O'Driscol, in his *History of Ireland*, that during the periods when the Catholics were predominant in that country, in the time of Mary, Charles the First, and James the Second, "*there never existed in that country a penal code against Protestantism. They made no law excluding their Protestant countrymen—a singular instance of moderation in Catholicity, while the whole history of Protestantism in Ireland is, in* THEORY, *liberty; in* PRACTICE, *intolerance.*" — "*It is,*" he adds, "*much to the credit of the Irish Catholics that, satisfied with a quiet and peaceable restoration of their faith, they in no instance persecuted or disturbed those who still thought proper to profess the religion of the Reformation.*" The learned and eloquent Parnell, speaking of the reign of Mary, says: "*Such was the general toleration of this reign in Ireland that many English Protestants took refuge in it; and there enjoyed their opinions, and worship, without molestation.*" — "*The Irish Roman Catholics,*" he adds, "*are the only sect that ever resumed power without exercising vengeance [...] And the reign of Mary closed, unstained by the crimes of any holy persecution in Ireland.*"

But is it, then, meant to assert or insinuate that Mary was not a persecutor? In Ireland, she was not. In England, unhappily, she was. And the Catholic condemns, and reprobates her cruelties, and her whole conduct in this regard, as much as does the most humane or bigoted Protestant. *She persecuted*; but then—for this is what alone I am now maintaining—

she did so, not in consequence, nor in virtue, of any tenet of her religion. In the instructions sent to her by the Pope for the regulation of her government, there is no exhortation to adopt any kind of severity or persecution. Burnet himself remarks that in the Synod, which was held in London by the Pope's Legate, Cardinal Pole, and the Catholic bishops, there was not any recommendation whatsoever to employ any kind of severity against the Protestants. Collier, indeed, remarks that the bishops, "*to do them justice,*" as he says, "*openly declared against these sanguinary methods; as did, also, Alphonsus, King Philip's Confessor.*" In the case even of Bonner and Gardener—the alleged authors and promoters of the cruelties which were exercised during this reign—it is nowhere so much as insinuated by either of them that they inflicted those severities in virtue of any doctrine of the Catholic Church. The sole reasons, and the only motives which those Prelates, and the other advocates for the measures of persecution, ever cited in vindication of their conduct, were exclusively founded upon the maxims of policy, and the pretences of necessity.

I would not seem to excuse, much less to justify, any part of the cruelties of the above persecutors. I consider their conduct as detestable, and, in fact, alike impolitic as detestable. However, it still cannot be denied that there were many circumstances and provocations which tend, in some measure, to extenuate their conduct. Mary, and her religion, were constantly and very grossly insulted. It was even at the risk of their lives that her clergy in many places ventured to exercise their functions. The whole conduct of the Protestant faction was violent and rebellious. This faction was composed of many of the leading nobility, gentry, and clergy who had conspired to dethrone the Queen, in the first instance, by setting up Jane Gray, and subsequently, by rising up in arms under the Duke of Suffolk and the rebel, Wyat. Mary's life was attempted, and her death was publicly prayed for; while books and pamphlets of the most seditious character were published and prodigally circulated against her—composed particularly by the refugees in Germany and Geneva, and by Knox, Goodman, &c. in Scotland. Such, and many such as these, were the provocations which, during the whole short career of her reign, the Protestants gave to Mary, to awake her anger and displeasure. They were far from justifying persecution; but they would have justified measures—even strong measures—of prudence and precaution. In regard of the horrible burning of Cranmer and his fellow Prelates, it may not be amiss to remark that they were condemned and executed by those very laws which themselves had enacted, and put in force, against the Anabaptists.

The argument, however, by which the Protestant writers most triumphantly affect to prove that the persecution of heretics is a tenet of the Catholic religion, is the Third Canon of the Fourth Council of Lateran. This is the argument which may be found repeated in all the above writers on the subject of persecution, and which is still loudly re-echoed from half the pulpits of the nation. Now, in the first place—in a merely critical point of view, it might be denied—as in fact it is denied by many Catholics—that the above Canon, relating to the persecution of heretics, is really the act or decree of the Council itself. "*Il est certain*," says Dupin—a favourite writer with Protestants—"*il est certain, que ces chapitres,*"—containing the Canon—"*ne sont pas l'Ouvrage du Concile, mais celui D'Innocent III*" ["it is certain that these chapters are not the Work of the Council, but that of Innocent III."] In the next place, it might be maintained—as, also it is maintained by several—that this Third Canon is not genuine. This is even the opinion of Collier. (Vol. i. p. 424). However, be all this as it may—for the aforesaid points are not essential to the question—the fact still is that the alleged Canon is neither defined, nor decreed, nor proposed, as a tenet, or as any article of Catholic faith. It is decreed and proposed simply as a matter of external discipline, enacted for a particular occasion, and adapted to a particular case or cause. Thus it is with many of the Canons of the Council of Trent relating to points of discipline. These are neither considered by the Catholics as articles of faith, nor were they ever, or at present, admitted in various kingdoms. So also with regard to the aforesaid Canon of Lateran, it neither is now, nor was it ever, looked upon by Catholics as any tenet of our religion—as in fact—the causes of its formation having long since ceased—it is now completely a dead letter.

It is, also, an observation which should be made in relation to the Fourth Council of Lateran, that it was not a merely ecclesiastical or spiritual Council. It was a Council, or Congress, of the Christian world—a *temporal* alike as a *clerical* convocation. It was called together and assembled for the welfare and peace of states, as well as for the protection and tranquillity of the Church. For this reason, besides the Prelates and members of the Church, there were present in it either personally, or by their ambassadors, the Kings of France, England, Hungary, Aragon, Sicily, the Emperors of Greece and Italy, the Princes of Jerusalem, Cyprus, &c. The aim and subject of their deliberations were how to arrest the progress, and suppress the mischiefs, of a heresy whose principles were as destructive of morality as they were ruinous of Christian piety. For, as Mosheim and many other Protestant historians admit, never did there exist a more impious, detestable, and seditious, sect than the Albigenses. The cause of the Council, in fact, was the cause of human nature, not less than of Christianity. At the same time, the decrees of the Council relating to these heretics extended only through the limits where they prevailed. Beyond these, or elsewhere, they were neither executed, nor yet molested.

Having thus shown that persecution for heresy *is not* a tenet of the Catholic Church, I will proceed to prove—grossly inconsistent as such doctrine is—that *it is* a Protestant tenet. The proofs are easy and incontestable. Thus, Luther, in language savage as that of a Marat, or a Robespierre, preached up persecution as a holy duty and obligation. "*Why,*" he called out, "*if men hang the thief upon the gallows; or if they put the rogue to death—why should not we, with all our strength, attack these Popes and Cardinals, these dregs of the Romish Sodom? Why not wash our hands in their blood?*" Zuinglius used the same kind of eloquence: "*Evangelium,*" he proclaimed, "*vult sanguinem.*" ["The Gospel wills blood."] And these words form the appropriate motto, and might justly be inscribed upon the banners of all the first leaders of the Protestant Revolution. They were, all of them, the defenders of persecution, both in theory and in practice. Even the gentle Melanchton wrote a book in defence of persecution.

I have stated already the sentiments of our English Reformer—Cranmer. He held the same doctrines as the above, and accordingly executed several miserable victims—burning Von Parris, Knell, Ann Askew, and condemning several others to the flames. It was so, too, with his chief fellow Prelates, Latimer and Ridley. They were, both of them, notorious persecutors.

At a subsequent period—in the tune of Elizabeth—Sandys, the Bishop of London, wrote a work in defence of persecution. And the dissenters, during this reign, attributed the persecutions which they underwent principally to the bishops,

The Fourth Letter

and above all to Parker, Aylmer, Sandys, and Whitgift.

In the reign of James the First, the pious Orthodoxy of the Parliament urged the use of persecution, "*as necessary to advance the glory of God.*" (Rushworth's Col. vol. i.) And the holy Archbishop, Abbot, concurring heartily in the same opinion, declared to James that "*to tolerate Catholics would be to draw down upon himself God's heavy wrath and indignation.*"

During the reign of the two Charleses, the solicitations of the Parliaments were urgent, and unceasing, to persecute the Catholics. "*To give any toleration to the Papists,*" said Archbishop Usher, in an address signed by eleven other bishops—"*is a grievous sin.*" Such, under every Protestant reign until that of George the Third, was, more or less, the spirit both of the state and the clergy. The laws of persecution, under every reign, went on increasing, and their execution—applauded by the bigotry of the public—was, at times, unceasing.

In Scotland, I need not state it, the employment of persecution was savagely inculcated by Knox, and his fellow apostles, Goodman, Willox, Buchanan, Black, &c., as "*a holy and sacred duty.*" The former of these barbarians maintained that "*the people were bound in conscience to put to death the Queen, along with all her priests.*" In 1560, the Scotch Parliament decreed the punishment of death against all Catholics, and they did it upon the principle that "*being,*" as they declared, "*idolaters, it was, consequently, a religious obligation to execute them.*" — "*With such indecent haste,*" says Robertson, "*did the very persons, who had just escaped ecclesiastical tyranny, proceed to imitate their example.*"

In short, referring to facts, and considering the whole history of Protestantism—this circumstance will be found accurately correct and true—that there is not so much as one single Protestant state, nor even town, in which, when the Protestants had once got the upper hand, they did not employ persecution and refuse toleration to the injured Catholics. "*The Reformation,*" says Rousseau, "*was intolerant from its cradle, and its founders were, all of them, a set of persecutors.*" Bayle, and even Jurieu, make the same assertion. Rousseau still farther observes that "*of all the sects of Christianity, Protestantism is the most intolerant and inconsistent, uniting in itself all the objections which it urges against the Church of Rome—whilst,*" he adds, "*Le grand argument de celle-ci lui manque—il est intolerant, sans scavoir pourquoi.*" [ED: Rousseau's original is "Elle est en particulier intolérante comme l'Eglise Romaine; mais le grand argument de celle-ci lui manque: elle est intolérante sans savoir pourquoi." "In particular, it is intolerant like the Roman Church; but it lacks the great argument of the latter: it is intolerant without knowing why."] In fact, if the liberty to judge and believe as each one's conscience dictates be the necessary right of every Christian, the dictate, both of reason, and religion—*as the Charter of Protestantism solemnly declares it is*, in this case, not only is persecution an act of inconsistency, but every restraint upon the alleged prerogative is a direct violation of the most fundamental law of the Reformation.

It is not by the way of defending the persecutions which the Catholics have, on any occasion, or under any pretext, inflicted upon the Protestants, that I will still here remark—that, comparing persecution with persecution, and the persecutions employed by the Catholics with those exercised by the Protestants—there is something—nay, there is much—to extenuate the guilt or excesses of the former, which cannot be alleged as an apology for the latter.

The Catholic, in his persecutions, acted in his own defence. For *his*, during the course of upwards of a thousand years, was the established religion of every Christian country—a religion, illustrious for its saints, its sages, and its heroes—a religion which, during that length of interval, had been everywhere the chief instrument of peace, virtue, and morality. *His* were the temples, the altars, all the riches, and establishments of the Church. All these were strictly *his*—fixed by the laws, sanctioned by prescription, and confirmed by everything that is most sacred in the order of religion. Therefore—although the measures of persecution are always wrong—still, as he but acted in defence of *his own*—every measure, *save persecution*, was, in him, but natural and consistent.

In regard of the Protestant persecutions, the case is extremely different. Here, the Protestants were the aggressors—complete revolutionists. They came forward with no claim but force—no title but violence, insult, and declamation. They introduced an entirely new order of things—new creeds, new principles, new practices. By artifice and plunder, they wrested from the hands of the ancient possessors the wealth and riches which these had enjoyed so quietly, for such length of ages, and to secure their triumphs, they persecuted cruelly the victims whom they had plundered. In the persecutions therefore thus inflicted by the Protestant, there is nothing to extenuate—as there is in those of the Catholic—the guilt and injustice of the odious practice. Put, for example, a similar kind of case in relation to a man's private estate—Who, I ask, is most in the wrong—the man who plunders, or he who defends his own property?

The eloquent, and amiable, the Rev. Sydney Smith—in the openness of his candour, makes nearly the same observations which I have done. "It is," he says,

> some extenuation of the Catholic excesses, that their religion was the religion of the whole of Europe when the innovation began. They were the ancient lords and masters of faith, before men introduced the practice of thinking for themselves in these matters. The Protestants have less excuse, who claimed the right of innovation, and then turned round upon other Protestants, who acted upon the same principle, or upon Catholics, who remained as they were, and visited them with all the cruelties which they had themselves so recently escaped.

Burnet himself remarks: "*Such was the conduct of the friends of the Reformation that it made all people conclude that it was for robbery, and not for reformation, that their zeal was made so active.*"

The Fifth Letter

Monsieur Le Comte,

WHEN you reflect upon the conduct of the English writers in their accounts of Spain, and particularly if you consider the intemperate but official condemnation passed upon it which I cited in my last letter, you cannot wonder that I should deem it proper to devote some observations to the awful imputations. The representatives of this great nation deserve, no doubt, to be listened to, when they pronounce an opinion in the midst of the national Senate. The English people—the first, beyond all dispute, of all other Protestant people—is, moreover, the only body of people that possesses a national voice, and that has the right of speaking out *as a people*. For these reasons, therefore, I think it useful to address them—and without being wanting in that respect, which they so justly merit—to ask them to render some account of their own faith. When you have viewed the state in which their boasted *liberty of conscience or toleration* has involved the nation, you will, perhaps, be reduced to own that this said liberty, as understood in England, is completely irreconcilable with any positive *faith* or belief whatsoever.

England tolerates *every* sect, and proscribes only *one* religion—the religion from which all its sects have been separated. Spain, on the contrary, admits only one religion, and proscribes all sects. How, then, can two fundamental laws, diametrically opposed to each other, be defended by the same means or arguments? The question is not to ascertain whether any coercive laws are required in order to leave each one the liberty of believing as he likes. This is a problem that is easily solved. The question is to know how any state without any laws of this description can maintain within itself any *oneness* of belief, or any unity of worship. And this is a problem which is not quite so easy.

The English reason strangely. Under the specious name of *liberty of conscience*, they establish an absolute indifference in regard to the doctrines of religion. And then, proceeding from this principle, they at once take upon themselves to judge and condemn those nations in whose eyes this indifference appears the greatest of misfortunes—if not even the greatest of crimes. But, they say, "*they are happy.*" Well, be it so—provided that unity of faith and the securities of salvation do not concern them. However, considering the two contrary suppositions—in what manner, I now ask, would their legislators proceed in order to satisfy this first will or maxim of legislation?

The Spaniard reasons as follows—"God has spoken. It is, therefore, ours to believe Him. The religion which he has established is *one*—precisely as He Himself is *one*. As truth is, of its own nature, intolerant, so, of course, to profess religious toleration, or liberty of belief, is, in reality, to admit and profess *doubt*—that is, to exclude *faith*. Woe, however, a thousand times, woe, to that stupid injustice which accuses us of damning anyone. It is God alone who damns. He has said to his envoys: '*Go; teach all nations. He that believes, shall be saved. He that believes not, shall be damned.*' Although penetrated with a sense of his goodness, we cannot, however, forget any one of his oracles. He cannot tolerate error, but we still know that He can *forgive* it. Therefore, we will never cease to recommend it to his mercies. We will never cease, both hoping everything for sincerity, and trembling at the thought that God alone is the witness to it."

Such is a Spaniard's profession of faith. Now, such profession, or such faith as this, supposes necessarily in its adepts a spirit of proselytism, and an insurmountable aversion to heresy and innovation. It implies a constant watchfulness over the artifices, and the projects, of impiety and incredulity, and a bold and indefatigable intrepidity in opposing them. In nations which profess this doctrine, legislation looks forward, above all, to the world to come—"*believing that all other things will be added to them.*"

How different from all this is the language and conduct of many other nations. "*Deorum injuriæ*" they say, "*Diis cura;*"—the injuries, offered to the Gods, is the concern of the Gods. Futurity to them is nothing. This brief and uncertain life absorbs all the cares and industry of their legislators. They are intent upon the improvements in the arts, and scienc-

The Fifth Letter

es, agriculture, trade, &c. They do not—dare not—expressly say—"*Religion is nothing to us*"—but their whole conduct implies it, and their whole legislation is tacitly *materialist*—since it does nothing for the soul, nothing for eternity.

Hence, then, there is nothing similar, or in common, between the two systems. Neither has the system of indifference any just reason to reproach the other, until such time as it can point out the means by which, without either vigilance or vigour, nations may enjoy security and repose. But this, alas, is a secret which will not easily be discovered.

And now look only at England itself—England, the boasted land of liberty, where men are forever preaching up the rights of conscience and the wisdom of toleration—look at its conduct when there was question or danger, as it pretended, with respect to its own Established Church. Hume has reproached its Inquisition, relating to the Catholics, as more terrible than that of Spain; because it exercised the same tyranny, without any of the order and forms of that tribunal. "*The whole tyranny of the Inquisition,*" says Hume, "*though without its order, was introduced into the kingdom.*"

Under the ferocious Elizabeth, the man who returned to the Church of Rome and the individua who reconciled anyone to it were, alike, declared guilty of high treason. Whoever, above the age of sixteen, refused, for a month, to attend the Protestant service, was thrown into prison. If he chanced to relapse, he was banished forever, and if he came back into the country—for example, to see his wife—or to attend a dying parent—he was condemned to be hanged as a traitor.

Father Campion, a man distinguished for his eloquence and learning, and for the sanctity of his life, was executed, during this reign, simply because he was a priest, and the comforter of his fellow brethren. Falsely accused of having entered into a conspiracy against the Queen, he was placed upon the rack, and tortured with so much cruelty that the gaoler, witnessing the inhumanity, remarked, that "the poor man would soon be half a foot longer."

Walpole, in like manner, was tried, racked, and executed. He was offered his pardon upon the scaffold, provided he would acknowledge the Queen's supremacy. He refused, and was hanged. (A).

And who is unacquainted with the frightful cruelties which, under this same reign, were exercised upon the Catholics in Ireland? "They were such as can neither be excused," say the

Edinburgh Reviewers, "by any principle, either of justice or necessity." Elizabeth was fully acquainted with them. There is still preserved among the archives of Trinity College, Dublin, a manuscript letter of an officer, named Lee, in which he candidly describes these horrors. "They are such," he says, "that one would rather expect to meet with them in a Turkish province, than in a province of England." — "And yet," says Cambden, "Elizabeth did not believe that the greater part of the priests who were thus condemned at her tribunals were guilty of any crime against the state."

In short, the code of the penal laws enacted against the Catholics—but, above all, in Ireland—form a system of oppression, of cruelty, and injustice unparalleled in the history of the universe. (B).

Bacon, in what he calls his *Natural History*, speaks very seriously of a certain magic ointment, composed, among other ingredients, of the united fat of a wild boar and a bear, killed, each of them, in the act itself of producing their young, and to this is to be added a certain moss which grows upon the skull of a human carcass that has been left unburied. As for the first ingredient, Bacon remarks, there might be some difficulty in procuring it in the way prescribed: but, in regard of the second, "This," he gravely, and without the slenderest expression of disgust, informs us—"This may be everywhere found, in great plenty, in Ireland, upon the carcasses which are thrown there, in heaps, upon the dunghills."

And let me here, my Lord, just make to you the remark that in a nation, the theatre of all this unrelenting persecution, it is a law, that "should the King ever embrace the Catholic religion, he would, by this act alone, forfeit his crown." This, although it is but the natural effect of that same intolerance, which I have been describing—this, *to me*, appears a very strange law: for thus, the parliament of England has the incontestable right of dethroning the very best of monarchs, if, prompted by piety and religion, he thinks proper to become a Catholic—and a Catholic King has no right whatsoever to drive away the meanest of his subjects if he thinks proper to become a Protestant.

Thus it is that nations fall into contradictions with themselves, and without perceiving it, render themselves ridiculous. An Englishman will prove to you very learnedly that his King has not the slenderest right of control over the consciences of his subjects, and that, if he were to attempt to restore the ancient worship, the nation would, in such case, have the right to depose him. But, if you were to say to this same Englishman—"How, then, did it happen that the eighth Henry, and Queen Elizabeth, had, in their times, a greater right over the consciences of the public than your Kings possess at present? And how comes it that the English, at the aforesaid periods, were guilty for having resisted two sovereigns, who, according to your English theology, were become, in relation to them, no other than real tyrants?" Interrogated in this manner, our Englishman would, no doubt, before he had seriously reflected—reply: "Oh, the cases are very different." Whereas, in fact, there is but one, and one incontestable, difference between them—namely, that the opponents of Henry and Elizabeth contended for the possession of sixteen centuries, whilst the present possessors are but the offspring of yesterday.

God forbid that I should wish to renew old quarrels. All I say is this—and I flatter myself, you will think, as I do—that the English are, perhaps, the very last people on earth that have any right to reproach Spain with its religious legislation. With more ample means of self-defence than is enjoyed by any other nation, the English have given themselves up to every form of horror and excess. They have murdered one king and expelled another; they have passed through all the convulsions of fanaticism and revolt ere they arrived at a state of tranquillity and repose. And how, then, with these scenes and reflections before him—how can any reasonable man presume to reproach Spain with "its *detestable Inquisition*"—whereas, at the same time, he cannot but know that Spain *alone*, by means of this Institution *alone*, traversed through two centuries of delirium, confusion, and crime, with a degree of wisdom that has extorted even the admiration of Voltaire.

Well has this same Voltaire remarked—although he has applied the maxim ill—that, "when a man's house is made of glass, he should be careful not to throw stones at the house of his neighbour."

But you may, perhaps, here observe that "the convulsions of England have now ceased; and that, although her present state may have cost her rivers of blood, she is now raised to a height of greatness which excites the envy and the admiration of all other nations."

To this I reply that no one is obliged, or even permitted, to purchase future, and uncertain, happiness, at the expense of great actual misfortunes and disorders. The sovereign who makes, or who is capable of making, such calculation as this, is alike criminal and rash. Wherefore, I think, that the Kings of Spain, who, by spilling a few drops of impure blood, prevented the effusion of torrents of the purest—I think they calculated wisely, and are undeserving of those reproaches which are so constantly cast upon them.

In the next place, I reply that the present state of England has cost the nation, not only *torrents of blood* but, what is still far worse—*the loss of faith*. England never ceased to persecute until she ceased to believe—a wonder this, which cannot well be boasted of. In the present age, it is the prevailing rule, although, indeed, the thing is done but tacitly—to act and reason upon the principle, or hypothesis, of materialism: and men, even the most reasonable, are, without being conscious of it, carried along with the torrent. If, indeed, this world be everything, and the next world nothing—then, I own, it is but consistent to do everything for the former, and nothing for the latter. But if the reverse be the case, and the next world is everything, and the present, comparatively speaking, nothing, then, also, it follows that the opposite maxim should be adopted.

England will, no doubt, say: "It is you, that have lost *faith*: and it is we, that are in the right." It surely requires no great ingenuity to answer this objection. Wherefore, I reply:

Prove to us, then, that you do really believe in your religion. And show us in what way you defend it.

There is no learned or well-informed person, but what knows, is really the fact, in relation to both the above subjects. For all that toleration which England boasts so much, is, at the bottom, neither more nor less than a system of downright indifferentism. It is true—the man who believes ought, of course to be charitable, but he cannot be tolerant without any restriction. If England tolerates everything, it is because she has no creed, save what is written upon the mere paper of her Thirty-nine Articles, (C).

If England possessed a system of fixed belief, she would then, in this case, esteem the various creeds of religion, in proportion as they resemble her own. But so far is this from being the fact, that she would a thousand times rather consent to be represented in her senates by a Socinian, or an unbeliever, than by a Catholic—proof this, that *faith*, to her, is a very immaterial object.

And since *faith* has thus visibly declined in England—or

The Fifth Letter

since rather, it exists no more—so has this nation, in all other regards so highly respectable—no right to criticise, or condemn, one which, looking upon the loss of *faith* as the greatest of misfortunes, adopts, therefore, certain measures to preserve it.

The more, Sir, you examine the matter, the more you will be convinced that what, in many places, men call "*Religion,*" is, in reality, nothing more nor less than the sheer hatred of Catholicity. This hatred is even sanctified under the terms of zeal, piety, faith, &c.—"*Dant nomen quodlibet illi.*" ["They give to it whatever name they please."][1]

We have lately heard an English bishop (the late Dr. Tomline) declare, in one of his charges, addressed to his clergy, that "*the Church of England is not Protestant.*" Strange and curious thesis! For, pray, then, what is it? "*It is*" replies the Prelate—"Scriptural"—which, in other words, means exactly this—that *the Church of England is not Protestant; but that it is Protestant.* For Protestantism consists essentially in nothing else, but in being *scriptural*—that is, in substituting the Bible in the room of authority.[2]

You may not have forgotten, perhaps, that in 1805 another English Prelate (Bishop Watson) was consulted by a certain lady of his acquaintance, respecting the important and difficult question—"*whether she could, in conscience, marry her daughter to a man who was not of the Church of England—al-*

---

1 One of the greatest statesmen of the present age, and a Protestant also, said to me one day: "*Without you, we should not exist.*" The sentiment was true, and deeply profound. He felt that the religion of all possible negatives is no other than the common hatred of the *affirmation*. If, then, you suppress the object of this hatred, what, I ask, remains? Nothing.

2 "*Our Church,*" says the bishop, "*is not Lutheran; it is not Calvinistlc; it is not Arminian*—It is Scriptural." Now, this is exactly what each and every Protestant sect will say of themselves. "*Our Church,*" says the Lutheran, "*is not Calvinistic; it is not Anglican; it is not Arminian*—It is Scriptural." And the Calvinist says: "*Our Church is not Lutheran; it is not Anglican, nor Arminian*—It is Scriptural." Thus, too, it is with all the rest of all the Protestant sects. They are all, and each of them, Scriptural. The sophism, although laughable, is, at the same time, honourable to the man who invented it—showing an uneasy conscience; and therefore, a more or less upright one—looking out for a shelter *somewhere*.

though neither a Catholic, nor a Protestant." (This alludes to Miss Button, the daughter of Lady Sherborne, who, soon after, married Prince ... a member of the Greek Church).

The reply of the bishop is curious. The learned Prelate establishes, in the first place, the grand distinction between the fundamental and unfundamental articles of faith: and he considers as Christians all those who maintain the former. In regard of the others, he says—"Everyone has his own conscience, and God is our Judge." He knew a gentleman, he adds, who had been educated at Eton and Cambridge, and who, after having carefully examined the grounds of the two religions, decided in favour of that of Rome. He does not blame him for this. And therefore, he thinks that the tender mother may, with the utmost safety of conscience, marry her daughter to a person who is not of the Church of England—although the children—the fruit of such marriage—were brought up in the religion of the husband. "If," concludes his Lordship—these are his words—"if, in every other respect, the match meets with her (the young lady's) approbation, and that of her parents, it must not be declined from any apprehension of her children's salvation being risked, by being educated in the Greek Church—ESPECIALLY (mark these words) as when they arrive at mature age, they will be at liberty to examine, and judge for themselves, which of all the Christian Churches is most suitable to the Gospel of Christ."

Such is the decision of the learned Prelate. In the mouth of a *bishop*, it is horrible. But in the mouth of an *Anglican* bishop, it is honourable. Had he even no other claim to the reputation which he enjoys, *it* alone is sufficient to conciliate for him the esteem of every respectable man. It most certainly does require a strength of mind, nobly independent—a nicety of conscience, peculiarly delicate—a degree of courage, extremely rare, to express, with that open frankness, which his Lordship has done—the presumed *equality* of all the various systems of religion—that is, in fact, *to admit* the NULLITY of his own.

Such is the faith of the bishops of that illustrious nation which ranks the foremost in the support of the Protestant cause. The former of those, whom I have cited, is ashamed of the origin of his Church, and wishes, and endeavours, to blot out its very name—that indelible name, which constitutes its essence—for, since its existence is grounded solely upon a *Protestation against authority*—so no diversity in the *Protes-*

The Fifth Letter

tation can alter or affect its essence. The Protestant Church, which once ceases to *protest*, ceases to exist.

The other Prelate, guided by the principle and rule of private judgment—which is the basis of Protestantism—deduces from them, with admirable honesty and frankness, a set of singular, but inevitable, consequences—of which the following is, in part, the real meaning—"Since one man does not possess any other power over the mind or opinions of another, save that of *syllogism*, (and this each one claims equally) so it follows that, beyond the exact sciences, there is no universal truth, and still less, no divine truth. The appeal to a book would be not only an error, but a piece of folly; because it is *of the book itself*, that there is question. If I believed, with *divine faith*, the doctrines which I teach—solely upon the authority of the King—I should, in this case, be highly culpable if I advised any parents to bring up their unhappy children in a state of error—reserving to them only the faculty of finding out the truth, when maturer age and increased learning had enabled them to judge for themselves. But the fact is—I don't believe these doctrines, or at all events, I only believe them with a human faith—just as I should believe in the system, for example, of Staalh, without attempting to hinder anyone from believing in that of Lavoisier—or just as I should see no reason why the chemist of one of these two schools should refuse his daughter to the partisan of the other."

Such as this is the precise meaning of the learned bishop's reply. It must be owned that honesty and consistency combined could not have expressed themselves better. But I again ask—where, and what, is faith, in a nation whose leading Pastors think and reason thus? or what possible ascendency or influence can they possess over the great body of the people—did but the people reason?

I have been acquainted with many Protestants, and particularly with many English Protestants, and I have made it my custom to study Protestantism in them. But never could I discover in them anything but so many theists, more or less improved and perfected by the Gospel. I found them utterly strangers to what is called "*faith*"—that is, divine, or divinised, belief. The mere opinion which they entertain of their own clergy is an infallible sign of the notions which they, also, entertain of the doctrines which they teach: for between these two things there exists a constant, and invariable, connexion.

I have traced, and observed, with a great deal of curiosity and attention, the manner in which the English in general die. Seldom attended by their clergy—whom, indeed, they seldom call for—they leave the world with little or no preparation to appear before the tribunal of their God—without any of those decisive acts of faith, hope, love, sorrow, &c., which the spirit of religion requires on so awful an occasion. I have found it thus even among many of the most celebrated characters of the nation. There was nothing in the deaths of these illustrious individuals that could either edify Christian piety, or that bespoke real Christian faith.

Another proof of the indifference of the English on the subject of religion may be traced in the manner with which their tribunals treat the offences committed against the presumed faith of their Established Church—but in the honours, still more, and the applause which nearly all the most learned portions of the community bestow upon the very enemies themselves of all religion—their Gibbons, Humes, Bolingbrokes, &c. Hume, for example, has exerted all his great talents to prove, "that it *is impossible, by human reason, to justify the character of God*." Gibbon, speaking of Rousseau's comparison between Jesus Christ and Socrates, observes—giving the preference to the latter—that "Rousseau had not paid attention to the circumstance, that Socrates did not suffer a word to escape him, either of impatience or despair." In fact, the works both of Hume and Gibbon are neither more nor less than, in general, a conspiracy against Christianity, and Christian piety. And yet they are everywhere read and admired.

I will cite, as an example of the criminal admiration paid to such works—and of the still more criminal indifference paid to religion—the conduct of the celebrated historian—Robertson. Robertson, although a preacher of Christianity, and an eminent theologian—with very unchristian politeness, complimented Gibbon upon his writings—nay, he even prostituted his praises upon Voltaire, and requested the pious Madame Du Deffant to express to him "*the extreme respect and veneration*" which he entertained for the great philosopher.

I ought not to omit the observation that whilst England is thus tolerant to infidelity, and to every form of heresy and sectarism—to the Catholic Church she is still intolerant and unjust. The English dislike a system which enjoins them to

The Fifth Letter

believe *more*, and the man is sure to be well received who proposes to them to believe *less*. The nation swarms with dissenting sects, which undermine and destroy its Established Church—leaving to it little else than a certain form, which some, as yet, take for a reality. Sensible of this, and in order, if possible, to stay the torrent, several writers—and these, too, members of the Established Church—have proposed—by softening down certain articles of its creed—to enlarge the pale of this Institution, so as to admit into it Christians of every denomination. This is, no doubt, an admirable expedient; and the persons who propose it, reason but consistently. Dogmas matter little. The creed of the Anglican Church is reduced to a mere line, and that line is the first. Beyond this, everything is mere opinion and sentiment. Whence, it is my conviction that, as a *religious* establishment, or a *spiritual* power—the Church of England exists no longer. Two centuries have sufficed to reduce the trunk of the worm-eaten tree to dust. The bark alone remains, because it is the interest of the civil power to preserve it.

I have the honour to be, &c.

Notes and Illustrations.

(A.)—The English Penal Laws against Catholics.

WHOEVER will seriously consider, and candidly compare, laws with laws, and punishments with punishments, will be reduced to own that the penal laws of this country against the Catholics were more severe and unjust, and the execution of them, on the whole, more frequent and distressing, than what we now reprobate so much in the laws and the cruelties of the Inquisition. He will find that the English Protestant has been a greater persecutor than the Spanish Catholic. Consulting our Penal Statutes against Popery, he will be reduced to feel that there is nothing in the Codes, either of a Nero or of any other tyrant, against Christianity that comes up to them in point of injustice, inhumanity, and oppression. "*They are a system,*" says Mr. Burke, "*as well fitted for the debasement of human nature itself, as ever proceeded from the perverted ingenuity of man.*" In fact, they are the violation of every principle, both human, and divine—of every law, moral, social, natural, and Christian. I will cite only a certain portion of them: for such was their multitude and variety that they followed and pursued the Catholic through every path, and at every step, of life, from the cradle itself to the grave. For example,

The Catholic, by these laws, was declared, and made, guilty of *high treason*, for the following causes—for refusing to take the oath of supremacy; for maintaining the Pope's spiritual power; for giving, or receiving, absolution; for being reconciled to the Catholic religion; for receiving Holy Orders beyond the sea. For these alleged offences, he was condemned to be hanged, cut down alive, and while still living, to have his bowels ripped open and burnt before his eyes.

He incurred the penalty, and punishments, of *felony*—for receiving, or concealing, a priest; for returning from banishment; for leaving the kingdom without having taken the oath of allegiance.

By a variety of absurd acts, he was subject to a *præmunire*—for example, for the receipt of a crucifix, or a pair of beads!

He was, by a multitude of unjust and odious laws, condemned to various *disabilities* and *vexations*. He could hold no office, either civil or military. He could neither be an executor, nor an administrator, nor a guardian. He was confined

The Fifth Letter

to the limits of five miles within his dwelling: and if he passed those limits, he was condemned to forfeit all his goods, and his copyhold lands might be seized.

He was exposed to numberless *forfeitures and seizures*. These were, indeed, constantly recurring, and they formed not only a source of oppression, but often of absolute poverty and ruin. Thus, if any Catholic presented himself at Court; or came from the country into the City of London, he incurred the penalty of a hundred pounds, and was, moreover, considered as excommunicated, in regard of all personal actions, and disabled from either maintaining, or defending, a personal action or suit. If he married according to the Catholic Rite, he was to forfeit a hundred pounds. And in case that his wife was convicted of recusancy, he forfeited for her, every month, ten pounds; or else, one third part of his own remaining third part of his property. And again, if she survived her husband, she could neither be his executrix, nor his administratrix: she was to forfeit, moreover, two parts of her jointure, and two of her dower. She might, likewise, during her marriage, be taken away from her husband, by any Justice of Peace, and be confined in his house, till she conformed.

If a Catholic christened his child according to the Catholic rite, he forfeited a hundred pounds. At nine years of age, his children might be presented, and at sixteen, indicted, for recusancy. If he kept a Catholic schoolmaster for the education of his children, he forfeited, for each day, forty shillings: and if he sent them abroad, he forfeited a hundred pounds—whilst, also, the children thus educated could neither inherit any lands by descent, nor purchase, until they had conformed.

If a Catholic harboured, maintained, or relieved any recusant servant, sojourner, or stranger—his father and mother excepted—he forfeited, for every month, ten pounds. In short, the system of persecution, as I have said, followed and pursued the Catholic from the cradle to the grave. For, if he were buried in any other place but the church, his executors were condemned to forfeit twenty pounds. Such as these were some of the worse than barbarous laws which, until yesterday, composed the penal code of this country against the Catholics.

In regard of the execution of these laws, it will be easily conceived that the men who had the cruelty and injustice to enact them would have, also, the savage consistency to execute them. Accordingly, such likewise was the case. During the frightful length of four successive reigns in particular, they were executed and enforced with a degree of cruelty and injustice that would have done credit to the most brutal tyrants of Turkey or Algiers.

During the reign of Queen Elizabeth, there were put to death, (I state the numbers from the eloquent Sydney Smith's "*Letter to the Electors*,") two hundred and four Catholics. Of these, one hundred and forty-two were priests; three were ladies; and the rest, either gentlemen of ancient families, or respectable yeomen. Besides these, there died in prison ninety priests and laymen; whilst a hundred and five were mercifully condemned to banishment, and to the loss of their entire property. The fines, and forfeitures, and seizures during the whole reign were such as to reduce multitudes of families—and many of these the most opulent and honourable—to a state of absolute poverty and distress.

"With respect to the great part of the Catholic victims," adds the same candid writer,

> the law was fully and literally executed. After being hanged up, they were cut down alive; dismembered; ripped up; and their bowels burnt before their faces: after which they were beheaded and quartered. The time employed in this butchery was very considerable, and in one instance, lasted more than half an hour.

He, moreover, adds that, "*In the list of the Catholic victims, no person is included who was executed for any plot, real, or imaginary, except eleven, who suffered for the pretended plot at Rheims—a plot which was so daring a forgery that even Camden allows the sufferers to have been political victims.*"

As farther instances of the barbarity with which the laws were executed, the same writer adduces the cruelties exercised upon Father Southwell; and three respectable and harmless females—ladies of distinguished rank. "*Southwell*," he says,

> *was racked ten times, during the reign of the sister of the bloody Mary. Mrs. Ward was hanged, drawn, and quartered for assisting a Catholic priest to escape in a box. Mrs. Lyne suffered the same punishment for harbouring a priest. Mrs. Clitheroe was accused of relieving a priest; and she was pressed to death,* (between

two boards) *in York Castle—a sharp stone being placed underneath her back.*

The accounts which Cardinal Allen, in his "*Modest Defence*," has given of the various methods of seducing and punishing the Catholics during this reign are, some of them, even more disgusting and atrocious than the foregoing instances. Thus, he tells us that, in order to withdraw them from their religion—"*Many innocent virgins were placed under the care of strumpets, to be corrupted—that children were taken away from their parents, and placed under the tuition of Protestant instructors—that the ears of some priests were burnt; and those of some others cut off—and that many were cruelly whipped.*" In short, he adds; "*There were committed unspeakable horrors, not inferior to any of the Pagan persecutions.*"

It is not possible to ascertain, at present, the multitude of Catholics who, in different towns and places, heroically suffered for the cause of their religion. Dr. Bridgewater, indeed, published an account of twelve hundred of these victims, who, by various means, fell a sacrifice to the cruelty of their persecutors, even during the periods of comparative lenity—that is, previously to the year 1588. Thus, Mr. Sydney Smith, whom I have cited so often, says: "*I find fifty gentlemen lying prisoners in York Castle.*" (They were all thrown in there, in one single night.) "*Most of them perished there, of vermin, famine, hunger, thirst, damp, dirt, fever, whipping, and broken hearts. They were, every week, for a twelvemonth together, dragged by main force to hear the established service performed in the Castle Chapel. The Catholics were frequently, during the reign of Elizabeth, tortured in the most dreadful manner.*"

I think, then, as the Count De Maistre asserts, that no nation has less right to reproach Spain, or any other Catholic country, with the injustice and iniquity of persecution than England. I think it even historically true that there suffered a far greater number of Catholics during the reign of the "Virgin Queen" than there had suffered Protestants during that of the "bloody Mary."[3]

---

3 As Protestantism was a real Revolution, so wherever its advocates had once attained power, they uniformly became the persecutors—even the cruel persecutors—of the Catholics. This will be found true in every country where Protestantism prevailed, or attempted to prevail, over the ancient religion. Thus, for example, in France, the

During the reign of the First James, the number of the Huguenots not only prohibited the exercise of the Catholic worship, but they everywhere murdered all the priests and religious who fell into their hands. Fromenteau, one of their own historians, relates that in the Province of Dauphiny alone, they slaughtered two hundred and fifty-six priests, and one hundred and twelve religious. The brutal cruelty of their leader, the Baron D'Adrets, is well known. He employed every form of punishment that his savage character could invent. For example, having taken the Castles of Montbrison and Mornas, he forced the Catholic prisoners to leap down from the towers, so as to fall upon the pikes of his soldiers, whom he had ranged around the walls. It is even asserted by his historians that, in order to render his children cruel like himself, he compelled them to bathe in the blood of the murdered Catholics.

In Holland, the cruelties exercised by the triumphant party of the Protestants were similar to those employed by the Huguenots in France. Wherever the soldiers of the Prince of Orange, particularly those commanded by his two distinguished lieutenants, Vandermerk and Sonoi—wherever they carried their victories, they uniformly put to death every priest and religious who fell into their hands. Such was the case at Dort, Middleburg, Delft, Ondenard, and Shonoven. Feller asserts that Vandermerk slaughtered more priests and unoffending peasants in 1572 than ever the Duke of Alva had executed Protestants during the whole course of his administration. Kerroux, a Protestant historian, relates some of the cruelties which Sonoi exercised upon the Catholics in North Holland. He tells us that some of these, after having been scourged and racked, were wrapped up in sheets that had been steeped in the spirits of wine; and that in these—being set on fire—they were actually burnt to death. Others, he informs us, after having been tortured with burning sulphur, and with torches, applied to the tenderest parts of the body, were made to die from the want of sleep—having executioners placed over them, in order, by additional torments, to keep them awake, whenever nature, through exhaustion, appeared ready to sink into sleep. He again relates that many were fed with nothing but salted herrings—without one drop of water, or of any liquid—until they expired and died of thirst. Some, he adds, were stung to death by wasps; some devoured alive by rats—some destroyed by cruelties too indecent to be described.

I think, it may be doubted whether the burnings inflicted by Mary in Smithfield; or those of the Quemadero in Spain, were, in reality, more cruel and atrocious than the hangings by Elizabeth at Tyburn, where the victim was cut down alive, his bowels in this state ripped

Catholics who were executed for the exercise of their religion is very inferior to the multitude of the victims who were put to death by Elizabeth. James was not, by inclination, a persecutor. He was rendered such only by the bigotry of the times. The numbers he put to death were *only* twenty-five—of whom eighteen were priests; the rest respectable, and pious, laymen. But, then—save this merciful fact of not sending, like Elizabeth, hosts of Catholics to the gallows—he, in all other regards, exercised against them, like the Virgin Queen, the most unjust severities and oppressions. He prohibited the exercise of their religion—he exiled a hundred and twenty-eight individuals, and he crowded the prisons with others. Thus, in 1621, when there was question of Charles's marriage with the Princess of Spain, James requested the judges to relax a somewhat in the persecution of the Catholics. And there were, accordingly, says Prynne, let out of the dungeons and prisons four thousand of these victims. To these hardships there were also added, and constantly executed, various other penalties of the law—fines, seizures, confiscations, disabilities, &c. So that the reign of James was, in reality—such was the spirit of the times, and the iniquity of the laws—a reign of cruel persecution.

During the reign of Charles, and the duration of the Commonwealth, there were put to death, on account of their religion—just as in the reign of James—*only* twenty-three Catholics. Such is the computation assigned in the letter of Mr. Sydney Smith.

The reign of Charles was a reign of religious fanaticism—so much so, as Hume observes, "that it confounded all ease, safety, interest; and dissolved every moral and civil obligation." This fanaticism, however, was directed almost exclusively against the Catholics, whose situation and sufferings, during a considerable part of it, were awful and distressing in the extreme. Not even would the Lords, and Commons, as Hume states, under any consideration, allow the Queen to hear mass. They passed a vote, he says, declaring, "that out of their detestation of that abominable idolatry used in the mass, they could not admit, or consent to any indulgence in any law for exempting the Queen from the penalties, enacted against the exercise of the mass." — "Every accident," he again adds,

open, and cast before his eyes into the fire, &c.

> that befell, if unpleasing, was attributed to the counsel of the Papists and their adherents. This expression, which recurred then every moment in speeches and memorials, begat at that time the deepest and most real consternation throughout the kingdom. The pulpits resounded with the dangers which threatened religion from the desperate attempts of the Papists. All stories of plots, however ridiculous, were willingly attended to; and dispersed among the multitude […] Alarms were, every day, given of new conspiracies. The Papists had entered into a plot to blow up the river with gunpowder, in order to drown the city. So violent was the bigotry of the times that it was thought a sufficient reason for disqualifying even a Protestant from holding any office, that his wife, or relations, or companions, were Papists […] Hayward, a Justice of Peace, chanced to be wounded by a Catholic madman, and this enormity was ascribed to Popery, not to the phrensy of the assassin. And great alarms seized the nation, and the parliament.

Under these circumstances, it is easy to imagine what must have been the situation of the Catholics. Petition upon petition was presented to the parliament for their punishment: and address upon address was presented to the King for the rigid execution of the penal laws against them. Accordingly, such was the fact. They were everywhere hunted after, like so many wild beasts, and the prisons and dungeons were everywhere crowded with them. Godwin, in his "*Lives of the Philipses*," says: "It has been computed that sixty thousand persons suffered, on a religious account, under the persecutions of Lord Clarendon; and that, of this number, five thousand perished in prison." Of these the far larger proportion were, of course, the hated and persecuted Catholics. Hume, indeed, tells us that "some were murdered, merely on *suspicion* of being Papists." I say nothing of the losses, the seizures, the confiscations, &c., which the Catholics, during this reign, were compelled to undergo. Every possible art of injustice and tyranny was practised and enforced against them. The reign of Charles was, again, a reign of persecution. And yet—astonishing fact—it was in defence of this prince that ere long—in the midst of his own trials and persecutions—the

The Fifth Letter

Catholics—the whole body nearly of the nobility and gentry who had survived the injuries of the times—generously came forward—sacrificing for his sake, who had so little deserved it—their lives, their fortunes, and every domestic comfort.

Under the Commonwealth, I need not say it, every injustice was practised against the Catholics which had been exercised during the reign of Charles—confiscations, fines, imprisonments, &c. Their treatment was even, in many instances, still more severe; because Cromwell was indignant, and deeply incensed, against the whole body, for the zeal and courage with which they had opposed his usurpation; and for their devotion to the cause of the murdered monarch.

During the reign of the Second Charles, Mr. Sydney Smith states that only eight Catholics—they were priests—were put to death for their religion. The number is probably underrated. For, Hume states, that "Charles allowed several priests to be put to death, for no other crime than their having received orders in the Romish Church." But be this as it may, all those other modes of persecution were enforced and practised which had been adopted and followed since the reign of Mary. The most atrocious act of persecution, however, which marks this reign—and which, in point of iniquity has hardly a parallel in any other—nay, says Mr. Godwin, "hardly a parallel in point of systematic and deliberate injustice, in any other age or country"—was the tragedy of Oates's Plot.

In order to prepare the way for this iniquitous event, "Rewards," says Hume, "were offered and given to any wretch that would come forward and accuse the Catholics. And though they possessed neither character sufficient to gain belief even for truth; nor sense to invent a credible falsehood, they were caressed, rewarded, and supported." — "By these atrocious proceedings, accompanied by calm and undaunted perjuries, there were committed," says Godwin, "the most execrable murders, under all the forms of law; but with the grossest violations on the part of the judges who presided, with whom it was, at all times, a sufficient reason for giving no credit to a witness—that he was a Catholic […] There were destroyed," he adds, "on this occasion, twenty innocent men; (all Catholics, of course) and twice as many, in the darkness and misery of a prison."

Since the foregoing reign, there has not been executed, in this country, any Catholic priest, for the mere exercise of his religion—although some have been imprisoned and tried upon this account. They were acquitted only through the ingenuity and humanity of the judge. The penal laws still continued, until yesterday, to disgrace and defile our statute book; and it was only after the persevering and generous efforts; and by the triumphant eloquence of one portion of the legislature that, at length, the repeal of them was extorted from the reluctant assent of an illiberal ministry. Until this happy epoch, the sword of Damocles still hung over our heads, supported but by a thread, which any miscreant or informer had the power to cut and let fall upon them. We were, moreover, still subject to a countless variety of hardships, injustices, and privations—a mere caste, deprived of our rights, as men, as citizens, and as Christians—degraded, insulted, and reviled.

However, those gloomy days have passed away: and the beams of justice and liberality have, at length, shone upon this nation in our regard—dispelling many of those clouds of bigotry, prejudice, and intolerance which, for three centuries, had disgraced it. They have shone even upon some of those palaces where hardly a ray of charity towards the Catholic had ever smiled before. (They shine not, indeed, Exeter, upon thine. There a spirit, like that of Abbot, whose chief religion was the hatred of Popery, sits sullenly frowning down indignation upon our heads.) But above all, mercy, justice, and liberality are now seated, in their most lovely forms, upon the throne; and its steps are occupied by men, the proper representatives of such a sovereign—men of great minds, and of generous hearts—enlightened, just, liberal, and benevolent. "*Mercy, and truth, have,*" at length, "*met each other. Justice, and peace, have kissed.*"

(B.) *The Irish Penal Laws against Catholics.*

Describing the general character of these laws, Mr. Burke says of them:

> Their declared object was to reduce the Catholics to a miserable populace, without property, without estimation, without education […] They divided the nation into two distinct bodies, without common interest, sympathy, or connexion, one which was to possess all the franchises, all the property, all the education—the others were to be drawers of water and cutters of turf for them […]

"*It is truly,*" he adds, "*a barbarous system, where all the parts are an outrage to the laws of humanity and the rights of nature.*"

In like manner, Dr. Johnson, speaking of the execution of these laws, declares that "*There is no instance, even in the ten persecutions, of such severity as that which has been exercised over the Catholics of Ireland.*" Indeed, the sad story of persecuted Ireland might be well written upon a roll, like that visioned by the Prophet Ezekiel—inscribed, both within, and without—"*Woe.*"

The savage and unjust laws which I have described as forming a portion of our English penal code, were, of course, common also to Ireland. For which reason I need not repeat them in this note. There were, however, beyond these, certain others which were, more or less, peculiar to that country; and of which, therefore, I will state a few. For example,

No Catholic could hold any office in any city, walled town, or corporation.

No Catholic, whether peer or commoner, could take a seat in either House of Parliament, under the penalty of five hundred pounds; and of being subject to all the punishments of a popish recusant. He could neither hold any office whatsoever—neither sue, nor defend himself, in action of law—neither be an executor, guardian, &c.

He could hold no office, nor receive any salary, or pay, unless he first took the oaths of supremacy, made the declaration against transubstantiation, the mass, &c.; and moreover, received the sacrament publicly—under the penalty of five hundred pounds.

He could neither keep any school, nor send his children abroad for education.

A younger brother, by conforming, might deprive his elder brother of the legal rights of primogeniture, and even his very parents of their estates.

No Catholic could be the guardian, nor have the tuition or custody of any child under the age of twenty-one. The guardianship was disposed of by the Chancellor to the nearest Protestant relation; or else, to some other Protestant, who was required to bring up the child in the Protestant religion.

If any Catholic priest chanced to marry, although inadvertently, two Protestants, or even a Catholic and a Protestant—unless they had previously been married by a Protestant minister—he was liable to suffer death.

No Catholic was allowed to keep any firearms, although it

was for the defence of his own life, or the protection of his property. It was even made penal for him to cut his victuals with a knife exceeding a certain length of blade. Every maker of firearms was forbidden to take any Catholic apprentice, under the penalty of twenty pounds upon the master, and the same sum upon the apprentice.

No Catholic was allowed to keep a horse exceeding the value of five pounds.

No Protestant was permitted to marry any Catholic who had an estate in Ireland.

No Catholic was allowed to purchase any freehold property.

All advowsons possessed by Catholics were vested in the Crown.

No Catholic was allowed to take an annuity for life.

Whoever had conformed to the Protestant religion, and held any office, was required to educate his children Protestants.

The widow of a Catholic, turning Protestant, was allowed a portion of her husband's property, notwithstanding any will to the contrary.

Every Catholic schoolmaster and usher were ordered to be prosecuted as regular popish convicts.

Every priest, turning Protestant, was allowed an annuity of thirty pounds, to be levied and paid by the grand juries.

There was a fixed scale of rewards from fifty pounds to ten for discovering Catholic priests and schoolmasters.

Any two Justices were empowered to summon any Catholic above eighteen years of age and commit him to jail for one year, or until he paid a fine of twenty pounds, if he refused to tell where and when he heard mass celebrated, and what persons attended it, or to mention the abode of any Catholic priest or schoolmaster.

No one was permitted to undertake any trust for any Catholic.

No Catholic was allowed to take any more than two apprentices, except for the linen trade.

In the year 1705, it was ordained by the House of Commons that "all magistrates, and other persons whatsoever, who omitted to put the penal laws in due execution, were betrayers of the liberties of the country. And a vote was passed that the prosecuting and informing against Papists was an honourable service to government."

Even so late as during the reigns of the first two Georges,

The Fifth Letter

although all the aforesaid laws remained in force, there were still added to them others which, if not equally barbarous, were yet, in a high degree, insulting and unjust. Thus, during the reign of the first George, it was enacted,

That the horses of the Catholics should be seized for the militia—that the Catholics should pay double of the Protestants, and that they should find Protestant substitutes:

That no Catholic should be either a high or a petty constable, nor be permitted to vote at any vestry:

That Catholics resident in towns should be obliged, under certain penalties, to provide a Protestant watchman to watch in their room. Under the second George, the following laws were made:

That no Catholic should be allowed to vote at any election unless he had first taken the oath of supremacy:

That Protestant barristers or solicitors, marrying Catholics, should be subject to the same penalties as if they were Catholics themselves:

That persons robbed by privateers during a war with a Catholic state, should be reimbursed by a levy on the Catholic inhabitants of their neighbourhood:

That all marriages between Catholics and Protestants should be annulled, and that every Catholic priest, celebrating such a marriage, should be hanged.

Even so late as the year 1796, a law was made allowing all foreigners of every description—no matter what their religion—whether they were Jews, Muhammadans, or professed unbelievers—to become naturalised and free subjects upon taking the oaths of supremacy, &c. *The Catholic alone was excepted*—thus making the rejection of all religion a passport either to place or power, and rendering the pious adhesion of the Catholic to the religion of his forefathers a penalty and a crime.

Such as these were *some* of the laws—for I have by no means cited them all—which formed the penal code of Ireland—composed and enacted by the united wisdom and humanity of the English and Irish legislators. I have extracted them from the works of the two eloquent and patriotic Parnells. The former of these—the eloquent author of the "*Historical Apology*"—after having stated some of them, exclaims, with the feelings of a Christian and the indignant sentiments of a man:

> Oh! hearts of barbarians; of zealots—of Protestants! The flames which made the name of Bonner accursed—the hideous night of St. Bartholomew, are not so great a disgrace to man as your cold, contriving bigotry. Can we find terms strong enough to expose to Europe—everywhere else enlightened, and liberal—the dull, malignant conduct of the Irish and English Protestants?

Similar, too, to these are the terms in which—after having described the aforesaid laws—the equally eloquent Sir Henry Parnell expresses his generous and patriotic feelings. "*The penal statutes,*" he says,

> are now laid before the reader, under which the Catholics of Ireland so long and so patiently languished—statutes, unexampled for their inhumanity, their unwarrantableness, and their impolicy—which are adapted to exterminate a race of men already crushed and broken by the longest series of calamities which one nation ever had the opportunity of inflicting upon another. They were framed against Christians under the pretence of securing religion. They were the work of Protestants, than whom no sect has cried out more against persecution, when Protestants were the martyrs. They were sanctioned by a nation which owed its liberties, and by monarchs who owed their thrones, to a solemn covenant that such disabilities should never exist.

But I will now present a rapid and abridged account—extracted from the *Historical Apology* of the eloquent Wm. Parnell—of the manner in which, during a series of succeeding reigns, our monarchs continued to treat the Irish Catholics.

Under Edward the Sixth. "The objects of the English, in those days, were to gratify their avarice and pride—to pillage as well as to tyrannise."

Under Elizabeth. "The Protestant bigot, Sir Richard Cox, relates, *as a very meritorious action*, that Lord Mountjoy had reduced the Irish Papists to the necessity of *eating* one another."

"Sixty princes, independent, and exerting kingly prerogatives from time immemorial, were, in the course of six years, swept away from the face of the country by the energy of an ambitious woman."

"The priests were always murdered in cold blood whenever a town or garrison was taken."

"Valentine Brown calmly recommended the extirpation of the Irish Papists as the best means of advancing the Reformation."

"The Lord Deputy, Mountjoy, adopted the plan for reducing Ireland, pointed out by the Earl of Essex. This was by fire and by famine. No quarter was given in battle: and prisoners, taken in garrisons, were murdered in cold blood. Whole districts, from the smallest pretence, were delivered up to the sword. Because the Queen's troops could not kill fast enough, no Irishman was pardoned unless he undertook to murder his nearest friend or relation."

"If Queen Elizabeth had never been known but by her administration in Ireland, she might fairly have been ranked among the most oppressive tyrants that ever insulted the feelings, or outraged the interests, of mankind."

Under James the First. "Although James was known to have tampered with the court of Rome, yet, to please the Puritans, he prohibited the celebration of mass, and by a step still more brutal and proportionably stupid, he required the Catholics to attend the Protestant churches. Upon their refusal, the magistrates and chief citizens of Dublin were fined, and committed to prison."

"He condemned to death a priest of the name of Lalor; and expelled all the regulars from the Island."

"The confiscations were enormous. On the flight of the Earls of Tyrone, and Tyrconnel, he confiscated 500,000 acres. Sixty thousand acres were seized upon between the men of Arklow and Slane—three hundred and eighty-five thousand in the Counties of Leitrim, Longford, Westmeath, Leix, and Offaly."

"But at the latter end of his reign, he had recourse to an outrage which, for political villainy, can scarcely be paralleled. The lords and gentlemen of Connaught and Clare had compounded for their estates under Elizabeth; but had neglected to take out letters patent for the regrant of them. James, therefore, pronounced the titles defective, and claimed the estates as the property of the Crown."

Under Charles the First. "Charles, like his father, was not, by inclination, a persecutor. But, like him, from fear and policy, he became such. The injustices and oppressions which he exercised upon the Irish—his constant threats and frequent execution of the penal laws—his subserviency to the Puritans, whose hearts were hardened by fanaticism—whose power was commensurate to their hatred of the Catholics—who with one hand signed the law, and with the other raised the sword to exterminate the Papists—these, and such like causes, rendered the reign of Charles more tyrannical than that of his father, James."

"One of the acts of injustice, attempted by the unrelenting Lord Strafford, was the plan for confiscating the whole Province of Connaught. Here, the landed proprietors had already twice purchased their titles from the Crown—yet Strafford did not hesitate to outrage every feeling of humanity, and every rule of justice, by subverting them a third time. This transaction was certainly the most infamous act of oppression that was ever perpetrated by a plea of law, under the sanction of juries."

"Another important injustice was the perfidy of Charles, with regard to the celebrated graces. The Catholics had offered to pay one hundred and twenty thousand pounds for the enactment of certain laws for the security of toleration, property, and equitable justice. The King accepted their offer and gave his royal word that these laws should be passed. He took their money, and broke his word, and not one of these graces was ever granted."

"The Catholics were driven from the court, with every expression of contumely and contempt. The invidious fine upon them for not frequenting the Church on Sundays was perpetually threatened to be imposed, and at length, it was made a source of revenue, and was commuted by Lord Strafford for the sum of twenty thousand pounds."

It was owing to the above, and a thousand such like injustices and oppressions, that, goaded into despair, the Catholics did, at length, take up arms in their own defence. "But," observes the candid Parnell—"If it is certain that they became rebels, it is no less certain that their rebellion arose entirely from the injuries and insults inflicted on them. And if we have made this clear, it is unnecessary to carry the argument further—as this persecution was *increased* to a degree which future ages will scarcely believe—or believing, will wonder how it could be borne."

Such are a few of the accounts, and reflections, of the generous Parnell. His accounts, indeed, as well as his observations, are but similar to those which have been stated by several other Protestant historians and writers. Thus, Leland, for example, asserts, that "*The favourite object of the Irish Governors and the English Parliament was the* UTTER EXTERMINATION *of all the Catholic inhabitants of Ireland. Their estates were already marked out and allotted to the conquerors, so that they, and their posterity, were consigned to inevitable ruin.*" Warner—a Protestant clergyman—states nearly the same thing. "*It is evident,*" he says, "*from the Lords Justices' last letter to the Lieutenant, that they hoped for an* EXTERMINATION, *not of the mere Irish only, but of all the old English families, that were Roman Catholics.*" Clarendon even states that the Parliament party had absolutely sworn to extirpate the whole race of the Catholics. "*The Parliament party,*" he says, "*heaped many reproaches upon the King for his clemency to the Irish [...] the whole race whereof they had, upon the matter* SWORN TO EXTIRPATE."

During the Commonwealth. I need not attempt to describe the horrors of that dreadful period. They are known to every reader. In the whole annals of iniquity, there is nothing more atrocious. Every passion was let loose, and every crime committed, that the passions could either perpetrate or invent. Very justly does Mr. Burke say: "*No country, I believe, since the world began, suffered so much, on account of religion, as Ireland.*"

Speaking of the conduct of Cromwell and his brutal followers, Mr. O'Driscol says of them:

> Nothing in history is more dreadful than the slaughter committed by them when Ireland fell into their hands. They spared neither age, nor sex, nor infancy. There is little doubt that these gloomy fanatics imagined they would have sinned by sparing. It is probable that, like the Jews, when they spared a remnant of the people of Canaan, they considered any lenity to Popery as an offence that would be visited upon their children.

Hence, the savage murders at Drogheda, Wicklow, Cashel, &c. "At Tredah," says Hume, "the few who were saved by the soldiers, satiated with blood, were, next day, miserably butchered by the orders of Cromwell. One person alone of the garrison escaped to be the messenger of the universal havoc and destruction." Sir William Petty, indeed, states that between the years 1641 and 1652, "above five hundred thousand of the Irish were wasted by the sword, plague, famine, hardship, and banishment."

The system of spoliation and plunder, of course, kept pace with that of slaughter. "About five millions of acres," says Hume, "were divided, partly among the adventurers, partly among the English soldiers, who had arrears due to them. An order was even given to confine all the native Irish in the Province of Connaught, where they would be shut up by rivers, lakes, and mountains." They were imperiously commanded to retire into this most barren, and at that time, almost desolate part of the whole Island, on a certain day, under pain, if found beyond certain limits, of being killed like wild beasts.

During the Reign of William. During this reign, the system of spoliation was still carried on with the same unrelenting injustice and rapacity as heretofore. "So little," observes the eloquent author of *Captain Rock*,

> so little were the mere forms of decency observed by the rapacious spirit of the British government—which nothing but the confiscation of the whole Island could satisfy—and which having, in the reign of James the First, and at the Restoration—despoiled the natives of no less than ten millions, six hundred and thirty-six thousand, eight hundred and thirty-seven acres—now added to its plunder one million, sixty thousand, seven hundred and ninety-two acres more—being the amount, according to Lord Clare's calculation, of the whole superficial contents of the island.

To the injustice of the above conduct there was added that torrent of every form of iniquity which the armies of William poured out upon the country. "Every writer," says O'Driscol,

> who has treated of the affairs of this period has admitted the extraordinary depravity of this army. They confess that a flood of wickedness had been poured out upon the country by their 'deliverers,' of the most awful and appalling character—that no faith, nor promise, was observed—that murder, robbery, debauchery spread themselves over the country, and consumed and corrupted everything.

The Fifth Letter

Well, indeed, might Burke assert, that "*never did any country since the world began suffer so much on account of religion as Ireland.*" And never, he might have added, did any country since the world began exhibit so much patience. But "*cruelties,*" says the liberal Sydney Smith, "*exercised upon the Irish, go for nothing in English reasoning.*"

It might be supposed that in these days of comparative benevolence and humanity, there could hardly be yet found individuals, or at least, any considerable body of men, who would still wish to oppress and persecute the Catholic. However, such, I fear, is still even now the case. "There are persons," says the patriotic Moore, "who, at this moment, still sigh for the good old penal times—who consider liberality and justice to the Catholics a degeneracy from their ancestors, and who try to infuse into every remaining fragment of that polypus of persecution, the same pestilent life which pervaded the whole." Such, no doubt, is the spirit, and such the character of that powerful faction which still distracts and disgraces Ireland—the men who exhort their partisans "*to keep their powder dry;*" and who toast and cheer "the victory of the Diamond." Speaking of this dreadful faction, but a few years back, the eloquent writers of *The New Monthly Magazine* say of them—

> There they club their quota to propagate the rancorous overflowings of the vilest and most antisocial passions. There the ordained ministers of religion subscribe for the dissemination of the grossest and most mischievous falsehoods. There the magistrate chuckles privately over the libel which he is publicly bound to punish. There, to be pre-eminent in villainy, and matchless in audacity, is the short road to command sympathy, and to ensure subsistence. Narrow hearts, and narrow intellects, impervious to the more generous impulses of nature—oppressing those they fear, and fearing those they oppress—they too long have exerted their baleful influence in brutalising and debasing the Irish nation into permanent anarchy—creating the abuses which they now plead in justification of their own unpitying rigour.

Such, then, even now, is the general spirit of Irish Protestantism; and such the character of the men whom this spirit inspires. If, happily, now the bigots do not exercise the old long practised tyranny—persecuting and degrading the patient and insulted Catholic—it is owing, not to any feelings of charity or improved benevolence, but to the enlightened wisdom, and the new energies, of a government which, for the first time, has assumed the courage to resist oppression, and to hold, with steady hands, the sacred scales of justice. Under its auspices, then, we will confidently hope that, at length, the miseries of afflicted Ireland, will end—"*Dabit Deus his quoque finem.*" ["God will also give an end to these things."] We will hope that ere long that "wall of brass" will be destroyed which the hands of bigotry and injustice have erected between the Parent Church and the new religions. We will hope that even bigotry itself—become more enlightened—will subside into comparative—or rather, into real, benevolence; and that Ireland will become, in the order of nations, what it is designed and formed to be, in the order of nature—

"Great, glorious, and free, The first flower of the earth; the first gem of the sea."

(C.)—*The Protestant's Rule of Belief.*

THERE is nothing in the leading rule of the Protestant's belief that can impart that *certitude* which the character of *divine faith* requires; nor yet inspire that wise *conviction* which is so important to Christian happiness. On the contrary, there is nothing in this rule but what, if well analysed and consistently applied, must create *incertitude and doubt*—and what, therefore, must eventually tend to generate incredulity or indifference. These propositions—awful as they are—are, I conceive, as manifestly true in *theory*, as they are incontestably confirmed by *experience*.

For the mind to possess that *certitude*—that unhesitating certitude—which is the essential property of *divine faith*—or even enjoy that calm *conviction* which is the best ingredient of Christian happiness—it cannot but seem necessary that both its certitude and its conviction should be founded upon some firm and solid basis—upon principles so fixed, definite, and clear as neither to admit the misgivings of doubt, nor the fluctuations of instability. In fact, nothing should be so solid—as nothing is so solid—as the foundations of *divine faith*—nothing should be so secure and satisfactory as the

The Fifth Letter

grounds or motive upon which the confidences of Christian happiness repose. Without these requisites, the mind—whose very nature is weakness and instability, must necessarily be unsettled and perplexed.

And what, then, is the real and acknowledged foundation, both of the Protestant's faith and of his convictions? I am speaking of the *consistent* Protestant. The Protestant who forms his belief *consistently*, and according to his own rule of faith, is a man who, denying and rejecting the right of any external authority to decide or control his religious opinions—judges for himself, and forms his own system of belief, according to the dictates of his own reason and the suggestions of his own conscience. This alone is *consistent* Protestantism—insomuch that whatever Protestant has not formed his belief in this manner, is a direct violator of the first law of the Reformation.

In order, then, to perform the arduous task, the first expedient to which he has recourse—and in fact, the only one to which he should have recourse—is to study and consult his Bible. Accordingly, he does this. He reads, studies, and pores over the sacred volume—the book, alas, which, perhaps beyond any other, is the most difficult to understand. However, he reads and consults this. But then, here is the awful circumstance—his own weak and private reason is its only authorised interpreter: so that what forms his belief are the notions or opinions which his own judgment affixes to it. Wherefore, supposing any set of religious opinions formed in this manner—although formed with the utmost care and piety—can the person who has formed them thus be really, in his own heart, assured that they are certainly *divine*; the dictates of the Holy Ghost, and the solid basis of eternal security? Fanaticism, surely, or the boldest presumption, could alone confide in so palpable a delusion.[4] The peculiarity alone of a set

---

4 As an instance, how difficult it is for any private individual, however learned, talented, or pious he may be—to understand the Bible—the writers of the *Quarterly Review* adduce the example of Milton, on the occasion of his recently discovered work "*On Christian Doctrine.*"

"Milton," they observe,

> approached the sacred volume with reverential awe. He professed the most humble deference to its authority. He sought after the truth with conscientious care, and sol-

of opinions, or of a code of belief, formed in this manner; and—differing, as it must, from every other—cannot but destroy—to the good sense, at least, of every prudent man—the assurance that it is *divine*. In fact, any set of religious opinions that are formed and founded upon the judgment alone of any private individual, must, of course, be just alike uncertain, and alike unsteady, as is the judgment itself of the individual who presumes to decide. They can be no other than *conjectures*, or bare probabilities at best. And probabilities are not *faith*. And yet, such as the above is, alone, consistent Protestantism.

It is a fortunate thing for religion, as well as for society, that there are few *consistent* Protestants—few who, following their own leading rule, compose *by it* their own separate creeds. For if such were the case, there would necessarily be just as many creeds as individuals. The ordinary and general principle, therefore, of the belief of the great body of the Protestant public—for example, in relation to the Established Church—is habit, and the presumed authority of this Church. "*Perhaps*," says Mr. Secretary Knox, "*ninety-nine out of a hundred, have, from mere habit, belonged to the Church of England.*" This conjecture of the learned writer may possibly be exaggerated. But to believe, even upon the presumed or assumed *authority* of any Protestant church—this, besides being a violation of the first law of the Reformation—is at the same time a

> emn religiousness of manner. When, therefore, we inform our readers that the result of the whole work is a system of theology not merely in discordance with the Church of England, but with every sect by which we are divided—an incoherent and conflicting theory which combines Arianism, Anabaptism, Latitudinarianism, Quakerism—and we know not what to add, on account of his opinion on polygamy—but Muhammadanism. If then, such an intellect as Milton's, solemnly and exclusively directed to the study and development of the Scriptures, shall nevertheless have arrived at such conclusions—how shall humbler minds escape being blown about by every wind of doctrine, unless they forfeit their religious independence, and servilely addict themselves to the authority of their teachers?

No Catholic could, better than this, demonstrate the incompetency of private judgment to understand the Bible, and the necessity, therefore, of an unerring guide.

platform far too slender to form the basis of any belief that can be properly deemed *divine*. The reason is—and it is the acknowledgment of all the Protestant churches—that all churches, like all individuals, are liable to error, and that their doctrines consequently may be erroneous, and false. "*Articles of churches,*" says Bishop Watson, "*are not of divine authority. Have done with them. This* MAY *be true. This* MAY *be false.*"

However, so it is—nothing is so inconsistent as the Protestant churches, once powerfully established. For although all these profess to admit the rejection of authority or of all control on the subject of belief, as inconsistent with the liberty and the privileges both of the Gospel and of reason—yet they, all of them, claim a measure of authority, which is not, in fact, inferior to that of infallibility. Thus, for example, the Church of England commands and compels its members to believe its doctrines under the pain of excommunication. It even obliges its ministers to swear that they revere and accept them as the dictates of the Holy Ghost. Surely, if this is not inconsistency, and something worse, it is difficult to say what is.

But in order to show, still farther, how little the *authority* of any particular Protestant church—however powerful and respectable it may be—is entitled to be prudently regarded and reverenced as *divine*—let the reader only make the following simple observation. Let him take any single Protestant church he pleases—let him take, for instance, the Established Church of this country—a church which is, no doubt, distinguished for the learning, the talents, and the virtues of multitudes of its members. Let him take this church—behold, he sees, at once, that its authority is denied; and itself rejected as not being the true Church of Christ—by all the other Protestant churches and religions of the universe. Its authority is denied, and its pretensions, and creed, are rejected, by churches, perhaps equal to itself in point of extent and of the numbers of their members—for example, the whole Lutheran and Calvinistic communions. They are rejected, too, by men, who, in regard of learning, talents, and their exalted characters, are alike and equally famed, as are the members of the Established Church. Wherefore, considering these circumstances; and comparing authority with authority, and claims with claims—the inference, in the ordinary course of reasoning, is that the pretensions of the Church of England to any divine authority are groundless and unfounded. It is certainly so, if the concurrent and united judgment of a *larger*—and this equally enlightened—body of men be preferable to that of a *smaller*.

The foregoing consideration will appear still more forcible if to it be added, also, the reflection on the state of the Established Church itself. As described by some of its own members, "*it is shivered to pieces by wedges, made out of its own body.*" It is divided, indeed, into schools or sects, maintaining the most opposite and conflicting doctrines. "*We have*," says Mr. Nightingale, "*in the body of our clergy, Arminian, Calvinian, Unitarian, Pelagian, Arian, Socinian, Sabellian, Trinitarian, and I know not how many other sorts of Clergymen.*"—"*Attend,*" says Secretary Knox, "*to the controversy, at this day, within the Church of England, about the meaning of the 39 Articles; and the obligation, incurred by subscription. See, how some make absolutely nothing of this, or of them—turning the articles into a dead letter; and assent and consent, into a farce.*"

The public curiosity is, just now, excited by the formation of a new school or sect, which is rising up in one of the universities, and which is composed of some of its most learned, pious, and distinguished members. What, however, may be the real tenets, or the ulterior designs of these respectable personages, this is a secret which time must reveal. At present, they appear to be neither one thing nor another—*Via Medians*—wanderers between two very widely separated paths; too enlightened to approve of their own Church—too deeply prejudiced to make choice of ours. To ours, indeed, their leading and favourite principles would conduct them, had they but the courage to follow them up consistently. Whence, also, they are called by their own Protestant opponents, "*The Revivalists of Popery.*" But, Ah!—so, I fear much, it will be: arrived on the banks of the Rubicon, they will shrink back, and turn away. However, I will say: "*Tales cum sint Utinam nostri essent.*" ["So great they would be, if only they were ours."]

Concerning the private opinions entertained by multitudes of the most learned portions of the Established Church, I say nothing. These, of course, must be various and discordant wherever men reason and judge for themselves. If, indeed, the accusation, which is very frequently urged against them, be well founded—Socinianism is their favourite system. Hence, therefore, considering all the above circumstances—seeing the state of the Established Church, that it is thus divided within itself—rejected by all the other churches and sects of the Reformation, as well as by the immense body of the Catholic Church, considering these, and many such like circumstances—I cannot well conceive, how any prudent man can, upon *the sanctions of its* AUTHORITY, either adore its articles, as *divine*; or revere the establishment Itself, as the institution of the eternal wisdom. Here, again—just as in the case of judging by the *rule* of Protestantism—the prudent man must *doubt*.

If the evils resulting from the principles of Protestantism were confined but to certain doubts, concerning certain articles of faith; or if they were limited only to an inconsiderable portion of society, the misfortune, although great, would still be—comparatively speaking—of inferior moment. But, unhappily, both for the order of religion and of society, the great evils which result from those principles are these—that, besides producing doubts, and various forms of religious error—they produce, moreover—wherever they are boldly and consistently applied—either the rejection of all religion, or a total indifference to its doctrines. Such, certainly, is the fact: whilst, at the same time, the multitudes who do apply them thus are countless and innumerable—crowding all the paths of society, and consisting for the most part, of men—who, if not learned, are well educated. And then, what is still most awful—It is *by those principles alone* that they either defend, or pretend to prove, their respective codes of irreligion.

In fact, if once you emancipate the human mind from all restraint—if you proclaim—as the first law of Protestantism does—that every individual is the judge and arbiter of his own belief—why, with this prerogative—this "*Glorious Liberty of the Reformation*"—you may account at once—considering all the various forms of the human character—the force of men's passions, prejudices, and self-love; the differences of their capacity, dispositions, &c.—you may, considering these circumstances, account not only for every absurdity of error, but for every doctrine of irreligion, and for a total indifference to all religion. So obviously, in fact, are all these evils the natural and even necessary result of the aforesaid principles, that they were early foreseen and foretold by the very men who had introduced them. In their confidential letters to one another, it may be seen that the first reformers were frequently wont to own and to lament them. Thus, Melancthon, for example, in an epistle to one of his friends, says to him: "*It is much to be feared that the time will soon come when men will consider religion as a matter of no moment; or else they will look upon all differences of religion as mere trifles, and verbal things."* In another epistle, he exclaims: *"What a tragedy have we prepared for posterity!"* To foresee, indeed, and to foretell, all this—considering the above principles—required neither any great foresight, nor any prophetic spirit.

But, in order to ascertain how far, or how exactly, the predictions of Melancthon are verified, I recommend it to the reader to consult—for I shall not describe it—the state of religion in any or every country or place where Protestantism prevails. He will find that in them all his predictions are frightfully fulfilled. Thus, for example, describing the state of the Protestant Church in Germany, the learned Mr. Rose declares candidly as follows—*"The Protestant Church of Germany is the mere shadow of a name."* This description, if not literally true in regard of the Protestant churches everywhere, is still, it will be found, but too nearly correct in relation of them all. Infidelity, Socinianism, indifference are their prevailing characteristics, everywhere. Churches which were once so powerful and animated—formed by the hand of violence, and kept alive by the hatred and abuse of Popery are now dying away—little else than "the mere shadow of a name." In their exertions to pull down Catholicity, they have destroyed Christianity among themselves.

Even in this country—although the English mind is constitutionally religious; although the business of preaching never ends; and the Clergy are richly paid for their exertions and belief—even here, the spirit of incredulity, and indifference, are—if not general—very frightfully prevalent. *"In this country,"* says the Bishop of Durham, the late Dr. Barrington, *"there is an almost universal lukewarmness and indifference to the religion of Christ."* The late Bishop Tomline complains of the same misfortune. *"The characteristics,"* he says, *"of the present times are confessedly incredulity, and an unprecedented indifference to the religion of Christ."* Lamentations similar to these may be found in the charges of other prelates, and in the works of many of the pious defenders of the Established Church. The case is that the attachment to any church or religion must be—or at least should be, proportioned to the evidence of its truth, and to the force of the conviction which that evidence inspires. And there is nothing in the real character or grounds of the Established Church which, if well considered, either presents such evidence, or that imparts such conviction. Modern in its foundation—divided within itself—proposing articles which no one understands—professing, as every Protestant Church must profess, the wide principles of private judgment—it is not, considering these circumstances—to be wondered at that the public should entertain very slender attachment to it; or that, as Bishop Barrington laments, "*lukewarmness and indifference should be almost universal.*" If, indeed, multitudes still adhere—as there do—to the Established Church, it is not because they have, by serious study and investigation, convinced themselves of its divine character, but because they have not done this. Birth, habit, custom, fashion, interest, human respect—these are the general and the chief sources of their adhesion or attachment to it.

The men who now dignify themselves with the name of "philosophers," and who unhappily form an immense school in almost every country—all these are the ardent advocates and admirers of the Protestant rule of belief. It is precisely by it, as I have remarked already, that they all and each of them defend, and affect to prove, their respective systems of incredulity. They all reason exactly like the Protestant: and they contend that if the Protestant were but consistent, he would, with his principles, renounce, like themselves, the belief in revelation; and with them, adopt the system of pure rationalism—that is, of no religion at all. Thus, for example, analysing by these principles the progress of belief or opinion from the first rejection of the Catholic religion, through the different stages of error, down to the abyss of incredulity—the writers of the French Encyclopaedia reason, and conclude, as follows—"*The Catholic, Apostolic, and Roman, Church,*" they say,

> is incontestably the only safe Church [...] She, however, requires from her members the most entire submission of their reason. When, therefore, there is found in this communion a man of a restless and unsettled spirit whom it is not easy to satisfy, he begins, ere long, to set himself up as the judge of the doctrines proposed to his belief. Not finding in these that degree of evidence which the nature of them does not admit—he now makes himself a Protestant. However, soon discovering the incoherency of the principles which characterise Protestantism, he seeks for a solution of his doubts and perplexities in

Socinianism: and he becomes a Socinian. Between Socinianism and Deism there exists only a very imperceptible shade. The distance between them is but a step. And accordingly, he takes it. But as Deism itself is, again, an incoherent system, he insensibly precipitates himself into Pyrrhonism—a state of violence which is alike humiliating to self-love as it is incompatible with the nature of the human mind. He ends by falling into Atheism.

Such, according to the aforesaid writers, is the natural progress of error—conducted by the principles of Protestantism—from the rejection of Catholicity to the adoption of their own code of infidelity.—*Art. Unitaires.*

But at all events, the above writers contend and foretell that if the Protestants are not, by their principles, conducted to the abyss of Atheism, they must necessarily—provided only that they apply them consistently, become, ere long, Socinians. "Il faut," they say, "*qu'ils deviennent Sociniens—non,*" they add, "*pour l'honneur de leur religion, mais pour celui de leur Philosophie.*" ["They must become Socinians—not for the honour of their religion, but for that of their philosophy."] Accordingly, they remark:

> Il est certain, que les plus sages, les plus savans, et les plus éclairés d'entre les Protestans, se sont, depuis quelque tems, considérablement rapproches des dogmes des Antitrinitaires. Ajoutez à cela le Tolerantisme, et vous aurez le vraie cause des progrès rapides, que le Socinianisme a fait, de nos jours; des raçines profondes, qu'ila jetees dans la plus part des esprits—raçines, dont les ramifications, se dévellopant, et s'étendant continuellement, ne peuvent pas manquer de faire, bientôt, du Protestantisme en général un Socinianisme parfait, &c.

> ["It is certain that the wisest, the most learned, and the most enlightened of the Protestants have, for some time, been coming considerably closer to the dogmas of the Antitrinitarians. Add to this Tolerantism, and you have the real cause of the rapid progress which Socinianism has made in our days; of the deep roots which it has thrust into most minds—roots, the ramifications of which, develop-

The Fifth Letter

ing and extending continually, cannot fail to make, before long, Protestantism in general a perfect Socinianism, etc."]

The reasons which engage these writers—and they are equally the sentiments of the entire school—to entertain the aforesaid opinions, are these—They maintain that between the belief in the Catholic religion and the adoption of Socinianism—there exists no consistent medium—no fixed and settled rule upon which the mind can depend with confidence—no secure abode in which the heart can repose in peace. If reason, they say, is the sole judge and arbiter of men's belief—as Protestantism declares it is—then reason should admit and believe only what reason can comprehend. And hence, therefore, it is the concurrent opinion and concession of these writers that if there does exist a sacred code of revelation—or if the scheme of the Christian religion is divine—it can be so *only in the sense and according to the system of the Catholic Church*—because it is in this church alone that there exist any clear, definite, and decided principles. It is even for this very reason—that, hating religion as these men do, they direct all their efforts and employ all their talents, irony, and wit to overturn Catholicity—heedless of Protestantism with its thousand sects and inconsistencies.

Men may reason as they please—but no proposition can be more philosophically or more manifestly true than that the leading principles of the Reformation—the boasted prerogatives of Christian liberty—whenever or wherever they are adopted, and followed up with *consistency*, must always—and do always—conduct the mind to error; leading it from illusion to illusion—from precipice to precipice—until, at length, they plunge it into the abyss of Socinianism, or infidelity: or else, into a state of complete indifference. "*The thing*," says the candid Mr. Nightingale, "*is lamentable. But there is no way to prevent it, so long as the principle of the Reformation remains.*" The great evil of Protestantism is this, that, rejecting the principle of authority—it proclaims and renders every individual free and independent; and of course, the easy dupe of his own weaknesses, prejudices, or passions. It is a state of *nature*, wholly incompatible with any notion of Christian *unity*, or even of religious society. Protestantism is frequently compared to a maze or labyrinth without a clue. I should say that it might be still more aptly compared to an ocean without a shore—a sea without either anchorage or port—no star to guide the bewildered mariner; no landmark to point out his way. Hence, he is tossed about by every wind of doctrine, the sport of his own self-love, prejudices, and illusions.

To prevent the above evils there is but one remedy—but a remedy, alas, which in these days the Protestant is little disposed to adopt. *It is to return to that church whose principles alone are steady, unvarying, and clear.* Without such principles, it is alike morally and physically impossible that there should exist either any stability or any unity of faith—any fixed convictions, or any wise security. Without them, men must wander forever, bewildered and forlorn—like Noah's dove, "*which found no rest for the sole of her foot.*" It is true, indeed, that men may, without them, coalesce for some length of time; and the zeal of fanaticism, and the exertions of a richly paid clergy, may long continue to keep up and preserve certain established forms of worship. But gradually—as it is already the case in most of the Reformed Churches—these forms will alter; and like shadows, melt away. "*For,*" says Mr. Secretary Knox, "*incalculable vacillation is the natural effect of the leading principles of the Reformation.*" These principles, indeed, besides being thus the sources of "incalculable vacillation," are, moreover, levers too powerful to be controlled; and which must, in time, overturn the establishments themselves which are founded upon them. If, therefore, stability of belief and unity of faith be the necessary qualities, as they no doubt are—of real, and true, religion—or if wise conviction and calm security be the properties, as they equally are, of Christian happiness—then it is manifest that these blessings can nowhere be assuredly found and enjoyed, but within the sanctuary of that church whose principles are, alone, fixed and unvariable. "*La Religion Catholique,*" says the eloquent Terasson, "*est une Religion d'Autorité: et par cela méme, elle seule est une Religion de certitude, et de tranquillité.*" ["The Catholic Religion is a Religion of Authority: and by that very fact, it alone is a Religion of certainty, and of tranquillity."] Even the above cited Mr. Knox, although a Protestant—after stating the unfixedness of the principles of Protestantism—adds: "*And therefore the prudent man gladly listens to the voice of the Catholic Church.*"

THE END.

Studies in Reaction Series:

I	Jonathan Bowden	*Why I Am Not a Liberal*
II	Thomas Carlyle	*The Present Time*
III	George Fitzhugh	*Sociology for the South*
IV	Henry Sumner Maine	*Popular Government*
V	Sophocles	*Ajax*
VI	Numa Denis Fustel de Coulanges	*The Ancient Family*
VII		*Havamal*
VIII	Joseph de Maistre	*On the Spanish Inquisition*
IX	Nick Land	*The Dark Enlightenment*
X	Jean Bodin	*On Sovereignty*
XI	Livy	*Ab Urbe Condita, Book I*
XII		*The Wanderer and Other Old English Poetry*
XIII	Oswald Spengler	*Prussianism and Socialism*
XIV	Theodore Kaczynski	*Industrial Society and its Future*

www.ingramcontent.com/pod-product-compliance
Lightning Source LLC
Chambersburg PA
CBHW030041100526
44590CB00011B/288